SMART PARENTS SMARTER KIDS

A gold medallist, **Dr Pradeep Kapoor** (MBBS, MD) is a paediatrician based in Bhopal. He is an established name in the field of parenting, having written several highly successful books. His first book, *Make Your Child a Winner*, is a bestseller and has been translated into seven languages. His novel, *Fosla*, a humorous take on life in a medical college, is a rage among readers, both young and old.

A popular medical teacher, **Dr Neelkamal Kapoor** (MBBS, MD) is a professor and head of the Department of Pathology and Lab. Medicine at AIIMS, Bhopal. She is a WHO Fellow and also a Rotary GSE Fellow. Her book, *Commonsense Parenting*, is a big hit among parents. Besides her eminence in the field of medicine, she also writes stories, features and articles on health-related and other issues.

To her children, she is a very supportive, accepting and fun mother.

SMART PARENTS SMARTER KIDS
The New-age Parenting Guide

DR PRADEEP KAPOOR & DR NEELKAMAL KAPOOR

RUPA

Published by
Rupa Publications India Pvt. Ltd 2015
7/16, Ansari Road, Daryaganj
New Delhi 110002

Sales centres:
Allahabad Bengaluru Chennai
Hyderabad Jaipur Kathmandu
Kolkata Mumbai

Copyright © Dr Pradeep Kapoor and Dr Neelkamal Kapoor 2015

The views and opinions expressed in this book are the authors' own and the facts are as reported by them which have been verified to the extent possible, and the publishers are not in any way liable for the same.

All rights reserved.
No part of this publication may be reproduced, transmitted, or stored in a retrieval system, in any form or by any means, electronic, mechanical, photocopying, recording or otherwise, without the prior permission of the publisher.

ISBN: 978-81-291-3595-7

First impression 2015

10 9 8 7 6 5 4 3 2 1

The moral right of the authors has been asserted.

Typeset by SÜRYA, New Delhi

Printed at Thomson Press India Ltd., Faridabad

This book is sold subject to the condition that it shall not, by way of trade or otherwise, be lent, resold, hired out, or otherwise circulated, without the publisher's prior consent, in any form of binding or cover other than that in which it is published.

For Anvika, Avanee and Prateek,
who are the source of much pleasure and fulfilment in our lives

Contents

Introduction	ix
1. The Formative Years	1
2. Working Parents	15
3. Time Management	29
4. The Jury Is Still Out: Quality Time vs Quantity Time	41
5. Crèche—the Dear Friend	51
6. Talk to Them, Don't Talk Down	63
7. Punishment Doesn't Pay	73
8. Parent-Teacher Meeting—Making the Most of It	87
9. Hone Your Child's Talent	96
10. The Concept of Uniqueness	105
11. Group Activities Develop Bonding and Leadership	114
12. The Go, Grow, Glow Nutrients	121
13. Teaching at Home	138
14. Smart Parenting	152
15. CAN—Child Abuse and Neglect	165
16. Single Parenting	176
Acknowledgements	189

Introduction

From the joint family, to the nuclear family, to the new-age family—India has come a long way. With a whole new generation of parents, achievers themselves—graduates from IITs, IIMs and top medical schools—who want their children to outshine them, the sky is the limit. This new-age family believes in the philosophy—Shoot for the moon: even if you miss, you will land amongst stars.

An important factor working in favour of smart parents begetting smarter kids, is the rise of inter-caste marriages. The mixing of genetic material from two different pools, rejuvenates it and produces offspring with more potent and dynamic brains and bodies. If this strengthened genetic pool receives an optimal environment to develop, the results are bound to be phenomenal.

Parents have always wanted the best for their children, but now they seem more concerned and focused about doing the right things to foster their baby's growth and development, particularly of the brain. While a portion of a baby's hundred billion brain cells are prewired at birth, it is during the first five years of life that much of the essential wiring linked to learning, is laid down. Whatever happens during this period can have an enormous impact on how well the child learns and performs later in life.

But the story doesn't end here! How the child develops as a teenager, and what type of adult he or she finally becomes, is largely determined by the manner of parenting received throughout the preteens and teens. There is no denying that good parenting practices can play a key role in putting the child on the fast track to success.

There is no statistical definition of 'genius'; it is rather, more, a cultural term. 'Gifted' would be a better and politically more correct term to use. Gifted children are very rare, probably no more than 2 per cent of the population. It is their special abilities and creativity that puts them in this slot. Some parents enlist the help of child psychologists to determine giftedness, often through IQ testing. A high IQ score, though, is limited in its scope for predicting future success. Intelligence is 49 per cent genetic, and 51 per cent external stimulation.

Don't assume that smart kids are born smart. There are thousands of instances where it is presumed that the child would be a super success, but isn't. Then there are children who are written off, but who go on to climb great heights. It is the environmental (read: parental) influence that is the prime factor in the eventual success or failure of a child. Remember, you—the parent—are your child's best learning tool. It is traits like self-control, perseverance, and an ability to appreciate the perspective of others, which are crucial to reach the top. These are the areas where good parenting plays a vital role.

Parents must realise that every child is uniquely gifted. It is their responsibility to recognise their child's special talent, and to then nurture it. Engineer, doctor, teacher—the only three choices that existed till not so long ago—have given way to not less than a hundred viable and well-paid career paths. These days, career options are extremely wide and varied, and it is quite possible that the child will turn his/her talent into a profitable one.

Being a working parent is a challenging role. It involves a balancing act between meeting your child's needs for care and attention, for sharing a satisfying relationship with your partner and friends, for managing the homestead, and in being a reliable and competent employee—all this while also trying to enjoy life and parenthood. This is a simple statement but a tall order to execute, because it requires many and complex adjustments. However, if handled intelligently, it becomes a golden and most enjoyable period in your life, without affecting your career prospects.

We don't need any proof; we know that you are a smart parent. Your holding this book is proof enough! All we are attempting to do here, is to help you in your endeavour to make your kids smarter. Your goal is to help your child to be the best he or she can be, right? Then let's embark on this journey together...

Dr Pradeep Kapoor
Dr Neelkamal Kapoor

1
The Formative Years

The human baby has the slowest rate of growth and development amongst mammals. Therefore, she remains dependent upon her parents and caretakers for a prolonged span of time, providing ample opportunity to parents to shape the behaviour of their child. Once the young one develops independence and steps out of the home, external influences start modifying her responses. Her experiences widen and she no longer remains exclusively dependent upon parental inputs.

What this means is that parents should not let go of their primary and unique window of opportunity to lay a solid foundation for their child's future.

Ensuring their dominance in this world, humans have inherited a superior brain, which consists of billions of nerve cells with countless interconnecting pathways. Through an elaborate and complex network of nerves, the brain controls the functioning of the entire body.

Thus, the human brain provides a highly organised communication and computing network, which can store information, solve problems, and take decisions. The maturation of the brain is a continuous process, which starts at conception and gathers momentum after birth. This process bears a direct consequence on the holistic and staged development of bodily functions, providing the child with linguistic and social skills in addition to co-ordination.

The sequence of development—for example, learning to sit before walking—is the same in all children; but the rate or age at which they learn these functions varies considerably from child to child. Similarly, they must first produce sounds resembling vowels and consonants, before they can utter words and sentences; here again, the age at which different children accomplish this skill remains inconsistent. The factors responsible for these differentials are the genetic make-up and the environment, also known as the nature–nurture principle. Parents not only pass on their genes (nature), they also provide the environmental stimulation (nurture), especially during the most impressionable and formative years of life.

TIPS TO ACCELERATE DEVELOPMENT DURING THE FORMATIVE YEARS

1. Start talking to your baby as early as possible—from the intrauterine life-stage itself. Research has shown that even

at this most nascent stage, the foetus responds favourably to human sounds and music. When the mother talks to the baby comfortingly, or soft and soothing music is played, the baby's heartbeat becomes less rapid and more regular. We know of the story of Abhimanyu as described in the epic, Mahabharata: when he was in his mother's womb, he learnt to break through the army's ranks, in order to enter the 'chakravhyu'. So, whether you believe in new research, or old mythology, there is no denying the fact that early auditory stimulation enhances brain development.

2. To develop hand skills, let the child drink milk from a cup, and use a spoon to feed herself. Sit back patiently, and remain calm, because your little one is bound to be messy at first. Encourage her to stack up cubes and plastic cups. Broadly, a two-year-old should be able to build a tower of six cubes, and a three-year-old can stack up nine. Lego blocks, Meccano, and several other such games are ideal to train little hands to create simple structures At around four years, she will be able to copy a cross, write capital letters and draw a man with five parts. Give her old magazines and newspapers to cut pictures from.

3. Remember, children must be allowed to use the hand they prefer. Never force a left-handed child to become a right-hander. This can compromise the development of hand skills because the brain will receive confusing signals.

Do we need to remind you that Amitabh Bachchan signs the cheques for *Kaun Banega Karorepati* with a flourish of his left hand!

4. Development of linguistic skills is important for communication, a characteristic that differentiates humans from all other living beings. Initially, the child starts producing babbling sounds, followed by 'ba-ba, ma-ma, da-da' and so on. At around twelve to fifteen months, she starts imitating coughing sounds and speaks in a jargon difficult to comprehend. An eighteen-month-old can repeat simple words, and has a vocabulary of five to ten words. At around two years, she can combine two different words such as 'want biscuit', 'play ball'; and uses words like 'I', 'me', and 'your'. By the age of three, she is able to repeat numbers and rhymes.

Parents are generally quite conscious of any speech delay (whether perceived or real) and will rush their child to the paediatrician for a check-up. Fortunately, most of these worries turn out to be unfounded. There are, however, some genuine cases of speech delay which, if handled correctly at an early age, lead to almost normal development of speech.

Partial or total deafness is an important cause of delayed or absent speech. I know of a case where the parents first noticed that their six-month-old was not responding to the loud noise of firecrackers on Diwali night. The grandma declared the child to be extremely brave, but the mother was not convinced. She brought her to me for examination, and the baby was found to have a severe hearing defect. The history revealed that the mother had been administered Gentamycin injections during her pregnancy, presumably the cause of deafness in the child. Timely detection and early intervention, first in the form of a hearing aid, and then a cochlear implant, helped the child to develop her auditory faculties, and near normal speech.

Multilingualism, as a cause of delayed speech, has many supporters. Take the example of a south Indian family with a young child being relocated to the north of India. The child is faced with a vernacular language (Tamil, Telugu, Kannada, among others) at home, Hindi amongst her playmates, and English at school. Coping with three different languages may confuse the growing brain of the small child, leading to delays in the development of her speech faculties. However, in most instances, and soon enough, the brain is able to sort out these confusing signals and the child develops mastery over all three languages.

Picture books play a special role in the development of spoken language. Parents should use a variety of storybooks, with minimal text and plenty of visuals, to read out to their child while pointing out accompanying pictures. This provides her with double stimulation—auditory as well as visual—leading to a faster acquisition of language skills. It is not necessary to always stick to the story written in the book; you can use your imagination and make up a new story each time to keep the child interested.

Speech development depends mainly on environmental inputs. The more the parents and other adults in the family (grandparents and others) talk to the child, the faster she learns to speak. Unfortunately, the advent of nuclear families, especially where both parents are working, deprives children of this much-needed auditory input. On top of that, TV takes away most of the evening when the parents could have talked to the child instead. It is a universal phenomenon where a young child is forced to watch TV because the parents are parked in front of it.

Let's make it very clear—a young child cannot learn to speak by watching TV. This is because she watches only the visuals without really concentrating on the dialogue. A child's attention span is small, so she is drawn to the fast-moving advertisements, losing interest the moment the slow-winding serial/soap starts. So if you want your child to speak, switch off the idiot-box, and talk with her. Tell her stories, read to her from the picture books, sing into her ears.

5. The process of socialisation provides the child with the necessary skills to thrive in society. Each community operates in accordance with a set of rules that are passed on from one generation to the next. Later, at school, this helps the child assimilate seamlessly with her peers. On the other hand, failure to adhere to such social norms is considered variant behaviour, and the individual is treated as a social outcast. It is the duty of the parents to teach the basics of accepted social behaviour to their child.

Even a tiny infant develops an interest in her surroundings. She recognises her parents and is apprehensive of strangers. Between nine to twelve months of age, the child starts playing with family members and reciprocates affection. You should provide her with lots of love and attention, and always respond to her show of affection. Remember, children who don't receive love are seldom able to give love as adults. At fifteen months, the child can play simple ball games, and when commanded, rolls the ball to the other player. Domestic mimicry is a well-established form of social behaviour seen in children. They imitate simple actions such as reading, sweeping the floor, or washing utensils. You and your child can now become good friends. Colour and paint with her, read stories, and point to familiar objects. Always listen, and pay attention to your child.

A two-year-old child likes to move to music. She will play next to, but not with, other children. By three she may even share her toys with them. Between four and five, the child shows more independence and may visit a neighbour unescorted.

To function independently in society and at home, the child should be imbued with self-confidence. Allow her to choose her clothes, give her simple household chores, and show interest in what she has to say to you. Tell her as much about the world as you can, simply and honestly.

With the acquisition of linguistic capabilities, social skills and hand–body coordination, the basic tools needed for the child's personality development are in place. The personality is the final outcome of a complex interplay of three main components—heredity, environment and self-concept.

HEREDITY

Even very young babies reveal differences, not only in their behaviour, for example, sleep patterns, and feeding habits, but also in their reactions to a given set of stimuli. Some are startled at the slightest sounds, or cry if sunlight hits their faces; others are seemingly insensitive to such triggers. Thus, conditions that one baby can tolerate well may be quite upsetting to another.

These subtle differences in reactions and behaviour indicate that diverse personality traits are present from the time of birth itself, a manifestation of differing genetic endowments. Although these genes are most noticeable in our physical features such as the colour of our eyes and hair, shape of nose, build and complexion, they also appear to play a role in our reactions, and our sensitivity to various situations. Such tendencies are carried forward from infancy to young adulthood.

ENVIRONMENT

The basic personality inherited by the child is greatly influenced by the environment in which she lives. Her genetic inheritance interacts with, and is shaped by, the environmental factors operative in her world and, in fact, from the time she is a foetus in the womb. This interaction results in the emergence of a self-image or persona, which is responsible for directing her further development and behaviour. It has been observed that if a would-be mother gets proper rest, a nutritious diet and has a pleasant and happy pregnancy period, she gives birth to a healthy, happy baby who is well adjusted and less troublesome. The reverse is also true—an unhappy and strained pregnancy along with a poor diet results in a child who eats poorly, sleeps poorly, and has unsatisfactory weight gain.

A child is exposed to various interactions with other persons, typically beginning with the family, and going on to peer group members and other important people in constant and close contact with her. Much of her personality reflects experiences with these key persons. The child who is rejected and mistreated, is likely to develop quite differently from one who is encouraged and loved.

Why are some children reserved and shy, and others open and loving? Why do some run away from their homes, while others are adjusted to their family situation? Answers to these and several such questions can be found in the child's environment. The behaviour patterns children learn depend heavily on the role models they are exposed to; their socio-cultural environment is the source of differences, as well as of similarities, in personality development.

It's an undisputed fact of life that we can't escape the influences of our socio-cultural milieu. Our genetic endowment provides our potentialities for development, but the shaping of this potential—in terms of perceiving, thinking, feeling and acting—depends heavily on the inputs we receive from our physical and socio-cultural environment.

SELF-CONCEPT

In addition to heredity and environment, there is a third major aspect which shapes the process of personality development: the concept of 'self'. So far as is known, we are not born with any notion of 'selfhood', but as we grow, the concept of 'me', 'I', or 'self' is gradually established. The child starts using statements like 'I know', 'I want', and 'I will'. Several questions start cropping up in the child's mind:

- What kind of person am I? Am I good or bad?
- Is the surrounding world favourable to me, or against me?
- Who is my best friend?
- Does the teacher like me?

These apparently simple questions, can lead to extreme confusion if the child doesn't receive appropriate and positive inputs at home and in school. Parents and teachers should try to explain things in their proper perspective; a child's questions must never be left unanswered.

Gradually, the child starts exploring the possibility of changing or modifying things for the benefit of the self. Improving personal standing amongst peers as well as seniors becomes important to the child. A need to impress people is felt by all children at some stage of personality development. Such actions are essential for personal growth and social progress.

Still later, the child starts attaching values to actions, objects, and people. Concepts of right and wrong, good or bad, desirable and undesirable, start forming. Once the child has developed her frame of values, there is an attempt to defend them by rejecting new information that contradicts them. Through experiences, the child tends to form a self-image. If these experiences are positive and meaningful throughout her childhood, she develops a confident personality, feels secure, and has a sense of adequacy, competence, and self-worth. The reverse is also true, and the child who faces rejection and ridicule grows up with a poor self-image.

Finally, as the child develops a sense of selfhood she starts behaving in accordance with the norms as perceived and established by society. Thus, in addition to heredity and environment, the concept of 'self' has a strong sway over the course of personality development.

THE THREE CRUCIAL NEEDS DURING THE FORMATIVE YEARS

All children have certain essential emotional needs during their formative years, which must be met for proper psychological development to take place. These needs are inherent to all human beings and are as seminal for positive personality development, as nutrition is for healthy physical growth.

1. Security

The need for security remains with us all our lives. Lack of parental interaction and stimulation invariably leads to feelings of insecurity, which children are more vulnerable to in any case as they are not yet familiar with the world around them. If both parents are working, it is a good idea for them to adjust their working hours so that either one is at home at any given time, to look after their child. This will not always be possible; therefore, an attempt should be made to find a job nearer home, or vice versa. Later, when she starts going to school, ideally either parent should be around to receive her on her return.

Insecurity can also arise if the child has to cope with a domineering and demoralising peer group. Not knowing how to deal with a problematic issue can upset a child. Repeated exposures to unknown and apparently threatening situations may end in acute anxiety. Pervasive and chronic feelings of insecurity typically lead to fearfulness, apprehension, and failure to participate fully in one's world.

2. Love and belonging

'To love and to be loved', is the essence of all human life. Parental love and warmth remain the most important influencers for developing an assured approach to life. A sense of belonging is crucial to healthy personality development, and for effecting successful life adjustments. A loved child is a good achiever, and also more adept at tackling problems and finding solutions. It has been rightly said: 'one who is loved can't be poor'.

3. Values

A valueless child develops into a clueless adult. Values—as approved and accepted by society—must be instilled and reinforced repeatedly by the parents. The right way to raise a morally correct child is to lead by example. If you're honest, empathetic, truthful, and caring, that's what your children would most likely be too. If you lie, cheat, or curse, even though occasionally, you are sending wrong signals to her. When she is unable to find uniform value patterns, confusion sets in, and the unlimited energies of childhood remain underutilised. A sound value base leads to the development of competencies, a positive self-image, and a confident personality. Such a child ultimately succeeds, and the entire family, justifiably so, basks in her glory.

THE END PRODUCT

Development during the formative years is a complex process involving innumerable inputs (stimuli) and outputs (responses). The end products of this process are the qualities of 'independence', 'self-control' and 'competence'. It has been observed that children of working parents are more independent and self-assured than others, and are better able to cope with adverse situations.

By the age of four, most children have a fairly clear picture of themselves and their world. They become capable of discriminating, interpreting, and evaluating experiences, challenges, and situations. This makes it imperative that the early period of a child's life be maximally conducive for the emergence of a positive and confident personality. Children are our most valuable natural asset; let us try to mould this vast resource into an infinite treasure.

2
Working Parents

Neeti and Ravindran were brilliant scholars. Both were selected through intense competition to the premier national engineering institution situated in a metro city. In the first year itself they became part of an extremely cohesive group of friends—girls and boys from smaller towns; fun-loving, adventure-seeking, and hardworking. By the sixth semester Ravindran was sure that he wanted to spend his life with Neeti, but she took her time to decide.

They proceeded to join and complete an MBA course, take up jobs in two separate MNCs, and marry each other—all within a span of the next three years. Life went on like a dream, till their DINK (Double Income No Kids) status changed to that of DI & OK (Double Income and One Kid). It felt as though a fast-moving, well-tuned, and high-end vehicle had developed a rattle and, trying to change the course of its own volition, was now finding the steering in somebody else's hands.

Don't think, even for a moment, that they were upset about it; they loved their child and thought that it had brought a sense of purpose to their lives. Never ever had they imagined that they were capable of this kind of selfless love and concern for someone so tiny, yet so demanding. Neeti and Ravindran were always up to any task in the professional world—but would they stumble here, in the face of this lovable tyrant?

Being a working parent is a challenging role. It involves a balancing act between meeting your child's needs for care and attention, for sharing a satisfying relationship with your partner and friends, for looking after house and home, and in being a reliable and competent employee—all this while trying to enjoy life and parenthood. Now this simple statement is actually a tall order to execute because it also means subverting, or putting on the back-burner, your natural talents and career aspirations—if not permanently—at least for the time being. You are always pressed for time and a little low on energy, or VERY low on energy if you are a late-age parent. So what is the most logical way to manage this labour of love?

SETTING REALISTIC AND ACHIEVABLE GOALS FOR YOU AND YOUR FAMILY

The first thing to realise is that now you are a family—not two achievers living together in wedlock. Your thoughts, actions, and goals should be re-focused and set towards a strong mono unit, which is 'your family'. In the previous generation, the brunt of this realignment had to be borne by the mother either by instinct, or perforce, or even due to societal and family pressures. Now this rearrangement is more of a combine between the two partners. So the smart idea is to sit down to a discussion and to map out peacefully, in advance, your shared strategy for dealing with the situation.

The best time to do this is, in fact, while planning the pregnancy, rather than to have to face it head-on with anger and acrimony later. It is no different from having a business strategy meeting where the focus is on upscaling or downsizing one or the other operation or vertical for the benefit of the balance sheet. This is just to remind you that, in this case, the profit and loss account is your precious offspring. One may find this analogy a little mechanical, but let's not forget our goal of raising a smart kid, and who better to do this than smart, qualified, proficient parents.

Remember that the best blooms are a result of scientific nurturing, not those allowed to grow untended. The uncultivated garden is a confused weedy tangle of plants and underdeveloped, shrivelled blooms and leaves, which were unable to optimise their potential. Imagine so much resource going to waste only because the gardeners were too adamant against changing their old strategies, tactics, and attitudes.

MAKE LIFE EASIER BY ASKING FOR HELP

Now this is a tricky statement because it raises many questions. Do we really need help when so many parents have managed their little bundles on their own? God, having my mother-in-law all day round finding fault with my actions and pontificating on every issue! Aren't maids dirty? You know I've heard so many stories of maids downing the kid's milk and sharing their snacks? Just to enumerate a few instances...

If you are feeling confused, you are not the only parents in this quandary. Actually, it is tough to anticipate the event, and to know how much and what kind of help you would require. Most of the time, young parents over- or under-estimate the quantity and quality of support they would need. They are also unsure about who needs the help—the new mom, the kid, or the whole family. Insufficient help can lead to stress, sleep deprivation, and further physical or mental pain. This is more so in the case of the new mother, who may feel isolated, and exposed to the complete spectrum of post-partum (after childbirth) psychosis. This condition could lead not only to disharmony, but also to the breakdown of the family in the future.

Sona had it all planned out. While she was in hospital, she had her mother come to help, along with a maid to look after the baby. The maid stayed back when her mother returned home a month later. But another month passed, and Sona became more and more irked and perplexed. The brunt of her mood was borne by Aniruddh, her husband, who genuinely couldn't understand why this was happening. The baby was happy with the maid; Sona did the cooking so they were enjoying tasty, healthy, home-cooked food; her company provided very generous maternity benefits, with leave and a work-from-home option for up to three years…

One Sunday he suddenly realised what was wrong. He saw the emotions of longing and frustration in Sona's eyes while she was cooking and going about her household chores, which demanded a large chunk of her day. He realised that she ached to spend all her time with her baby, and to do everything for her herself, but it was the maid who was deriving those pleasures!

Gently, Aniruddh restructured it all. The maid was taught to cook; she was a little inept at the beginning but they managed through that period uncomplainingly. Sona now had the whole day with her baby—massaging her, playing with her, napping along with her, and awake and joyful when baby was up and chirpy. Calm and joy had descended on the household through diagnosing and solving the problem with a little manoeuvering.

CHANGING YOUR EXPECTATIONS AND PRIORITIES AROUND THE HOUSE AND ABOUT EACH OTHER

Now this is a big one. We are all used to a particular way of living, especially with regard to cleanliness, house management, and work- and leisure-related activities. When a child enters the home, all of this goes haywire. Now, the drawing room centre-table may have a big, sticky wet patch where the kiddo has spilled her orange juice. This would have happened earlier too, but you would have immediately cleaned it up because it was an unusual occurrence, and you mayn't have had any other more pressing chore at hand. But you have found that the moment you finished cleaning it up, there could be another spillage, with the cute devil grinning gleefully at this game, but which leaves *you* tired and despondent. In a few hours the wet spill becomes a dry patch, until you can finally get it off the table only three days later.

So dear Mom and Pop, no use getting worked up about it. Just grin and bear it till you get time to mop it off once the little one is asleep and you still have some energy left for the job.

Having kids does not change everything, but it does change a big part of your life. You won't be able to go out each night, watch every event on TV uninterrupted, or spend all of your free time solving sudoku puzzles. The so-called free time would be spent taking care of the tot. One may then ask—why have a baby? Well, when you sit down and think about this, you can have a hundred answers in a jiffy: with some as frivolous as 'I love the baby smell', to as serious as 'a child is the perfect image of God'. But perhaps all those answers can be compressed to one single thought—the creation of a child is a miracle! It begins as one cell, formed of equal halves of genetic material from the mother and the father. In nine months it transforms into billions of cells with specialised organ systems and a mind of its own. Consider this: zillions of people since ages past can't be wrong—having gone right ahead with it!

So you would need to be more flexible with your time, but become a less spur-of-the-moment person. You may need to get by with less sleep, but you and your spouse can take turns to have at least a decent shut-eye. As the child grows up and regularises her own sleep cycle, this issue will get resolved by itself. Sometimes you will feel that you have less time alone with each other, but if looked at with insight, you will see that, in fact, its all *three* of you that would become much closer.

Sometimes, with slightly older children, parents have unrealistic theoretical expectations. For example, if your friend's child has started walking by the age of one year, then you would expect yours to follow suit—one week over and you start agonising to death. Had the child been old enough with a complete vocabulary, she would have definitely told you guys to 'chill and give her a break'.

The environment of kids also has an impact on their behaviour, so you may be able to modify that behaviour to your liking by tweaking the environment. If you find yourself constantly saying 'no' or 'don't touch this' to your two-year-old, instead look for ways to restructure the house so that the surroundings contain fewer objects that are off-limits. This will cause less frustration for all of you.

BE REALISTIC

As your child grows, you'll gradually have to change your parenting style. What works with your poppet now won't work as well in a year or two, or with the second child either. So be very observant, and adapt yourself accordingly.

Parenting is a manageable job. Focus on the areas that need the most attention rather than trying to address everything all at once. If you are too tired to handle even that, take time out from parenting to do things that will make both of you happy. Remember, you can only make your little one happy if you are happy. Attending to your needs does not make you selfish; it simply means you care about your own well-being—another important value for your children to imbibe.

Many theories and experiences look good on paper, or during counselling sessions, but are impractical to follow in real time. Note that being a parent means growing up yourself first, and bringing order into your own personal life. If you were a smart parent you would definitely have order and discipline in your professional life too. You would understand that routine is important. Having an unpredictable lifestyle is time-consuming and unsettling for everyone. Young children become frustrated, overwhelmed, and rushed when their routines are inconsistent. Some suggestions to tackle these issues would be in order.

~

SOME PRACTICAL TIPS FOR WORKING PARENTS

If a survey were conducted amongst the smart young working set of parents, the most terrifying part of their day would turn out to be the morning. So, what can we do to deal with this? Well, the first and foremost suggestion is to give yourselves some extra time in the mornings. This is, of course, easier said than done; that urge to spend a few more minutes in your cosy bed is overpowering. The best way out is to gauge exactly how many hours of sleep you need. If it is seven hours, and you need to wake up at 6.30 a.m., then calculate backwards, and your bedtime would be 11.30 p.m. Now, it is important that you be very strict with yourself and get to sleep punctually, so that you can get up every morning with a refreshed mind and energised body.

The ancient advice still holds true: pack up your work and childcare bags before your night's sleep—this means you should ready the next day's attire the previous night, for yourself, and for your child. Get your child to bed early, ensuring she has adequate sleep, which is important for her development and growth.

Whichever parent has the duty to drop the kids to school, or to the bus stop, should use this time to connect with them. Don't be grumpy. Even if you are a late riser, or hate this chore, just shake yourself up, otherwise you will lose a valuable opportunity to communicate with your children. This does not mean a mere question-answer session; you can sing songs together, or be alert to the non-verbal clues your child gives out about liking or disliking a particular school event, teacher, or classmate. Most importantly, do not bring work stresses into this significant moment in time. Avoid conflicts in the morning—it is a no-win situation for all.

If you have to drop off your child on the way to work, then rethink the essentials to be completed before leaving the house each morning. To help, you can have a bedside diary in which you maintain a to-do list for the next day, since that memory is notable for failing you just when you need it most!

Consider an absolute no-TV-rule in the mornings. It is terribly distracting for everyone, and a sure-shot recipe for a delay in getting ready on time. This causes a volley of shouting, and a foul atmosphere at the start of the day, thus spoiling the mood for the rest of it.

FOOD, VICTUALS, RATIONS, CHOW...

Indian culture lays much stress on food; consequently, a great deal of time is invested in it on a daily basis. Issues of what to eat, and when to eat it, are pretty structured too. The system was well managed when we were agricultural joint families, with stay-at-home women. But now, working couples need to apply different food management techniques, without compromising on the nutritional value or quality of their meals.

Investing in a freezer, or a fridge with a large freeze compartment, is a good idea because one can cook double the required quantity, and freeze half for later use. On a day when both are late, or too tired to cook, you can thaw the food of your choice and enjoy a hot meal at your table.

You can also invest in a slow cooker, or rice cooker, and after putting in the ingredients, turn it on to cook before leaving for work. This will give you fresh, healthy, and nutritious food when you return home. Also, do give a thought to the fact that the menus need not be the same as what you have been used to before you had a child. For example, if you ate rice at lunch, and chapati with dinner, you could reverse it to suit your work schedule.

Although this has been reported ad nauseam, there is no harm in saying it again—depending on the age of the child, try and enjoy dinner around the table with the television off and all family members present. This is a good habit to cultivate because it provides a great opportunity for the family to interact.

SHOPPING SMART

No household can run properly unless some time is devoted to shopping for essential goods. You would definitely like to do this without your children but it is not always possible, especially in a nuclear family. Avoid taking tired and hungry children along because sometimes this can create a difficult situation in the market. Hence you need to look at ways out of this predicament and plan your shopping trip well in advance.

You can consider shopping online, or during the evening, or simpler still, ask your partner to do it. You can also plan big weekly shopping sprees, in which case having a shopping list is important. It can well be planned as a fun outing with some eating or gaming thrown in for those in your team who are bored by shopping.

CHILDREN GET SICK WHEN YOU LEAST EXPECT IT

When you are negotiating terms and conditions for your job, ensure that your employer and immediate boss know you are a parent, so if your child does get sick it is easier for you to take leave. Also make it known that in lieu of this facility, you would be giving your more than 100 per cent for the rest of the time.

You should also have a back-up plan in place, such as a

grandparent or a good friend, on standby. At the same time, try not to impinge on people too frequently: show your gratitude and definitely reciprocate the gesture with friends.

FAMILY HARMONY

Marienne Neifert says, 'The family is a perpetual source of encouragement, advocacy, assurance, and emotional refueling, that empowers a child to venture with confidence into the greater world, and to become all that he can be'. Excellent thought, but what does it mean in real terms? It simply means to not forget yourself, or your relationship with your spouse, and keep everybody connected. So it is important to make time for your partner in order to re-bond, re-blend, and to maintain a healthy relationship.

Go for a walk together, talk and listen to each other even if it is only for a short while. Do it even if you must have the pram in tow with a struggling baby in it ready to jump out. You can also plan regular, enjoyable, yet simple family activities that will provide your children with warm memories throughout their lives.

Most importantly do not forget yourself. Continue, or start, a regular exercise regimen, and do not completely let go of your hobbies. If it is not possible to do either with your partner, please go ahead on your own. Your own (and your partner's) good health and well-being is an essential part of your caring for both of you.

Numerous studies have been scientifically conducted to gauge the effect of working parents on their children's all-round well-being (satisfaction quotient resulting from tender loving care). Most have come to the conclusion that children are barely bothered about the apparent lack of time from their parents. However, they can always sense it if the parent is bringing work stresses home. So in other words, large chunks of togetherness time with a lot of stress, is worse than smaller amounts of happy and stress-free time spent with the child. In spite of this observation, it is important to analyse your own child's needs because every child, or human being, is different.

3

Time Management

Comedian George Burns said, 'Happiness is having a large, loving, caring, close-knit family...in another city.' It appears to be quite apt because oftentimes, while trying to manage jobs, kids, social responsibilities, and running a household, we tend to think along these very lines.

Anybody on this earth has only twenty-four hours, or 1440 minutes, or 86400 seconds, in hand every day of his or her life. Well, the figure in seconds seems to be more comforting when we talk of managing time, but the fact of the matter is that the time allotted is universal, wherever you may be, and in whatever phase of life you are. And, by the way, we hope you know that the word 'family' comes from Latin for 'servant'.

Why is time management important and necessary for a smart parent? Absolutely the same way it is important for a successful professional, because:

(1) Available time is limited.
(2) Time cannot be stored: if unused it is lost forever.
(3) One's goals are usually multiple, sometimes conflicting, and not all are of equal priority.
(4) Goals cannot be accomplished without the application of effort, which requires an intelligent use of time.

So, we need to understand that to be pronounced a successful smart parent of even smarter kids, we need to manage our time optimally. If this is not happening then we must dwell upon the issues that are preventing us from getting there. Perhaps it's our inherited traditions! India is a great country with immensely deep and trusted socio-cultural roots and behavioural patterns. Most of this generation of parents has been brought up amidst those undying mores; they are entrenched in them, or at the least, they continue to follow those customs and beliefs by rote. Hence, unintentionally, these cultural norms become the accepted way for parenting the future generation, and so it goes on. Let us explain it further through a well-known experiment:

A group of scientists placed six monkeys in a cage, and in its centre a ladder with bananas on top of it. Every time a monkey went up the ladder, the scientists dunked all the monkeys with cold water. Now, whenever a monkey tried to climb the ladder, the others would beat him up.

After some time, no monkey dared to ascend the ladder regardless of the bananas. The scientists then took one monkey out and put in a new one. The first thing this new monkey did was to rush up the ladder for the bananas. Immediately, the other monkeys beat him up. After several beatings, the new member learnt not to go up the ladder even though he had no idea why he was being beaten for it.

A second monkey was substituted, and the same sequence of events occurred. The first monkey also joined in beating the second one. The third, fourth, and fifth monkeys were changed, the beatings were repeated, and finally, the sixth monkey was replaced. Now, all six monkeys were new, and even though they had never received a cold shower, they continued to thrash any monkey attempting to climb the ladder.

If it were possible to ask the monkeys why they thrashed all those trying to go up the ladder, the answer would be…'We don't know the reason but that's how things are done.' Something similar happens in a young family nowadays. Normally, family members don't really know why they are doing things…(that belong to a bygone era and with relevance to a defunct lifestyle with its own related compulsions and accessories.) They only know that their parents, grandparents, and ancestors have been doing things this way forever, so it must be the only way to do them.

Jobs, professions, careers, homework, nappies, school dropoffs and pickups, grocery shopping, washing, drying, cooking, and a lot more...phew! This makes one feel out of control, with way too much to do, with not enough time to get it all done, and obviously, with barely any time to think, introspect, and analyse—leave alone to simply laze around.

So now the question arises: how to approach this dragon of a problem? The plan, theoretically, is very simple but a little difficult to implement.

- ✔ The first thing to do is to create an environment conducive to effectiveness
- ✔ Now set priorities, and start activities around them
- ✔ At the same time, begin the related process of reducing time-spend on non-priorities

The obstacles to managing your time usually boil down to over-extending yourself to the family, friends, work, volunteering, or complete inaction, for example, plonking in front of the TV, or chatting with friends.

WHAT ARE YOUR PRIORITIES?

Our frustrations often derive from spending too much time on unimportant activities, resulting in the neglect of the more critical things in our life. More often than not, important goals and activities are dictated or guided by external forces. However, it needs no reminder that for achieving happiness and contentment, only you can determine the goals and activities that are most crucial for you.

Getting started on this process is a boring prospect. It is tiresome to have to pull out a sheet of paper and a pen, or open a file on your computer, to list out your regular daily activities. But it needs to be done, and if done for three or four days, you will have an almost comprehensive list of your everyday chores.

Next, calculate the time devoted to each of these tasks. Besides listing the 'must do' jobs, also carve out time to brainstorm on issues, and to dream about the things you want to do for yourself—because these are important too, as important as oxygen is to life. Once you have this database in hand, you are all set to accomplish an optimal management of time.

Now, realign all the tasks on your list in the order of their priority for you, and your children. Once this is done, you start to regain control over your time and your life. But do not forget that these priorities are not frozen in time. They would assume high or low rankings depending on the phases of your life. So keep this painstakingly assembled database secure. Give it a relook from time to time. Add, subtract, or modify items from it as and when required.

For example, when your child is six months old, devoting your time to organising various weaning foods for her is a key task, but for an older child, helping with her delayed project work is more apt. It is vital here, to dilute her stress rather than to spend your time cooking her a four-course meal, which may even start an argument, or which she may throw up later, distressing you and other family members even further. Instead, one parent can organise a simpler meal, which is less time-consuming to prepare, and easy to digest too. Luckily, there are umpteen recipes available on the net, providing simple, nutritious, and healthy food.

'NO' IS A GOOD WORD

Saying 'yes' to everything is an enemy to good time management; saying 'no' comes easier to some people, but for most it is difficult. Sometimes it is a situational issue too...perhaps making it easier saying 'no' to your spouse than to your boss, as in the case of several other relationships too. A position of immense dilemma arises when we have to say 'no' in circumstances where we really want to say 'yes'. So, here again, your database comes into the picture. It allows you to use your priorities and goals to balance the incidental demands on your time and energies.

'No' can be said in many ways. Usually, a tactful 'no' is managed with a bit of negotiating skill. If you can't spend the entire day at school for your child's drama practice, say 'no', but offer to take sandwiches for lunch or tea, to the whole bunch of schoolmates, and their mums who have stayed on looking after their children, and yours. You can take the sandwiches across during your own office lunch or tea break. This task can also be shared between both parents—the one who gets a longer lunch break can make the sandwiches and the other who works closer to the school can deliver them. All it requires is a little pause, a deep breath, and a few moments of hard thinking to come up with such solutions.

At other times, practise being assertive and say 'no' to demands that don't match your priorities. You'll be amazed at how often people do understand, and don't take offence when you are honest about your reason for declining. It is the sly and crafty answers that hurt. Deceit can never be hidden, and that is why it is noticed and causes upset. You'll be surprised, also, at how liberating an honest 'NO' can be for you.

CHANGE THE RHYTHM OF YOUR DAYS

Time pressures are best managed by seeking balance and simplicity in our daily lives. We ought to learn to 'live in the moment'. If we are working, we should put our minds fully to the task before us. If we are resting, it is best to clear our mind from all thoughts, and focus on the pleasure of recreation. If we are playing with baby then we should give ourselves up completely to that enjoyment, with nothing else on our minds.

You can learn this art with a little practice. Notice the rhythm of your days—periods when you experience high or low energy; at best you can plan your day around these phases, your own natural tempos.

Nimisha would get up very early in the morning to complete her household duties before leaving for work, because she loved, and found peace, in a spick-and-span house. A few years of this schedule found her flagging, hence always irritated, and consequently in a perpetual crib-and-nag mood. One day it suddenly dawned on her that she actually hated getting up that early in the morning...but then, she did also crave that clean, neat, and organised house! Well, to cut a long story short, she reorganised her housekeeping schedule, to dusting and tidying at night before retiring to sleep, so she could have fifteen extra minutes in bed the next morning.

It also pleased her growing children who had started getting annoyed with the clatter of her very-early-morning house cleaning activities. When she mused over the reason for waking up at such ungodly hours to do these chores, it struck her that it was because her mom had done the exact same thing, and she had simply got conditioned into doing it too. But while her mother was a housewife, with time for a regular after-lunch nap to re-energise her—Nimisha's situation was diametrically opposite, with her 'busy-in-the-meeting' afternoons.

So we see that it is essential to stop and rest your mind and body regularly, even when you think you can keep going. Such a readjustment may also be necessary when you change your job, to adapt to the pace or pressure slots of the new workplace.

PLAN AND TAKE ACTION

Your priorities are set, and you've weeded out all unnecessary activities. Now, you need two calendars and a small notepad to help you make your plans.

The first calendar should show the months of the year at a glance. Write all your year-long commitments here, adding to them when you learn of a new 'must do' requirement. School schedules, holidays, project deadlines, due dates for large payments, important birthdays—as they come, jot them down in this calendar where they will be seen easily.

The second calendar is the monthly one. This can be maintained on a white or green board too (we find white boards less messy). Each new month, transfer the events for this period from your annual calendar to this one.

The third and final tool is your daily to-do list. Enlist your daily tasks in a notebook or small pad, and keep it in your bag for easy reference from time to time. Alternatively, you can use the memo function of your mobile phone, tablet, or laptop, or even the old-fashioned paper calendar for this purpose.

Take ten minutes at the end of each workday, or at night if you must, to write out your to-do list for the next day. Do not forget to strike off the tasks completed. You will feel exhilarated to see these strikethroughs. It is also helpful to take your spouse's schedules and calendar into account when planning your own.

The whole idea is to stop taxing your memory, instead leaving space in your mind for better uses. Writing down your various responsibilities is also the best way to clear your mind for relaxation, and for time-spend with your family. Remember, often, physical tiredness is easier to bear and to relieve, than mental exhaustion. Getting someone to massage your feet is still possible, but finding someone to massage your brain...impossible!

STOP MULTITASKING

Well...well...well...whether to multitask or not is a highly debated question. Especially when you are dealing with young kids. We would go in favour of one thing at a time, as it adds to your efficiency as a parent. Multitasking appears to be a very comforting thing to do; completing, or at least attempting, several jobs within a minimum time period is a beguiling thought. But when it comes to taking care of the kids—along with other tasks at hand—somehow they sense that you are not 100 per cent with them. This makes them cranky, and as they try to disrupt your other jobs, it gets you infuriated in turn.

It is also important to remember, while dealing with children, that there is a limit to what you can control (you can't push the mute button on a toddler). Hence, concentrate on those components that you *can* control. Turn off your email, silence your phone, sign out of your Facebook and Twitter accounts, and focus on the job at hand. Instead of attempting several things at once, plan your day so that you have blocks of time (even if only ten or fifteen minutes long) when you are working exclusively on one thing at a time.

TAKE ADVANTAGE OF THE GAPS OF TRANQUILLITY

The more you use your calendar, the more you'll notice those little time gaps, between slotted tasks, that are too short for anything substantial, but perfect for jobs and breaks of up to five minutes each. The secret is to have even little odd jobs and much-needed breaks queued up in your to-do list so you can wedge them into these gaps. Good 'filler' tasks include:

- Work-related phone calls and messages
- Checking on your social media networks—but if you find it difficult to stop, then its better you don't even start, or your calendar would go haywire
- Responding to email—but again, we offer you the same advice as above
- Personal care tasks that normally fall by the wayside (for example, nail care, stretching)
- Tidying up, even a single drawer, or surface, or floor area
- Sorting mail
- Filing papers
- Looking ahead in your calendar and to-do list to fine-tune plans (for example, noticing a birthday the

following week, so you mark a reminder on an earlier date in good time to buy a gift)

If thinking so much about time management is stressing you out, start planning a vacation. It could be long or short, a week or just a weekend, but do not take your calendars there; just enjoy your time out! Why do you think the travel and tourism industry is seeing a boom these days? Simply because every Nitin, Vinay, and Saurabh is doing this, with Vini, Barkha, and Nikita, along with Amaya, Kavya, and Arunav in tow.

4

The Jury Is Still Out: Quality Time vs Quantity Time

A heated debate was going on between Reshma and her mom who was visiting for a month. Her mother was extremely upset to see that although Toy and Joy, Reshma's young twin sons, were safe and secure, they didn't appear to be spending much time with their parents, both busy professionals. She was aghast at this situation, and when she communicated her displeasure to Reshma, an argument began. Reshma, on her part, was strongly defending her own and her husband's behaviour by saying that it is the quality of time parents spend with the child that matters. According to her mother, the more the time spent with the child, the better the parenting.

The proponents of the 'quality time' theory try to justify their limited interactions with their children by arguing that it is useless to sit in the same room with the child for two hours, engrossed in reading or watching TV.

If you play with your child or engage in some other interaction, even for thirty minutes, it is more beneficial.

Their opponents emphasise on the quantity of time spent with the child, as being of more value. They hold that you can't show the child your wristwatch and say, 'Your quality time of thirty minutes starts now, so enjoy it.'

Well, there is nothing new in this debate; it has been raging for almost half a century, and could perhaps continue eternally; but a deeper look into the phenomenon of time vis-à-vis parenting is of significance.

CHARACTERISING TIME

Quality time is seen as parents engaging with their children in particular activities, including outdoor excursions, which create and maintain family enjoyment, caring, and togetherness. Quantity time needs no explanations; after all, there are twenty-four hours in a day and all of them can be spent with their offspring. There are advocates for both positions in huge numbers and the debate is endless. Each party behaves in the manner they think right, and look down upon the other.

So you'll find 'n' number of Nehas and Poojas extolling the virtues of quantity time, the reason for the extreme sacrifice of quitting their jobs. You'll also find equal numbers of Nikitas and Ankitas, who work full-time, telling you about how independent and smart their kids are turning out to be, despite only weekends spent with them.

THE CHILD'S VIEWPOINT

The interesting thing is that this whole debate is entirely skewed to the viewpoint and perception of parents and other adults only. It completely forgets to include the standpoint of the child—how does he or she define quality time or quantity time? Also, not to forget that as the child grows older, her understanding and value of time changes too. Another question is whether it is only the parents who constitute the useful and happy rainbow time spectrum for the child, or is it also the friends, or grandparents, or someone else who could enter this ambit too...

So let us first view this conundrum from the child's perspective. Many studies have been conducted, especially in the western world, regarding the entity of time and its relationship with parenting. One important aspect discovered was that modern families actually have a little more time with their children, because of better organised work schedules, faster means of transportation, and fewer children. So what emerges is that it is not an issue of definitions of time, but of finding better ways to approach time with reference to parenting.

When this issue is looked into more scientifically, it can be gathered that children value five aspects of time spent at home and/or with the family. They are:

a) Family time as ordinariness and routine
b) Family time as someone being there for you

c) Having a say over one's time
d) Time for peace and quiet
e) Being able to plan one's own time

a) The value of family time as ordinariness and routine

The Kumars—that is Pratul, his wife Sameeksha, and their children Nimiti and Niyati, love watching the daily soap on television at 9 p.m. For half an hour they are stuck to the couch in front of the TV, not talking and if possible not even blinking. We agree this is most unusual in today's era, what with a remote control device at the ready! Usually one TV with multiple watchers means deep trouble, with each one trying to switch to their favourite channel. Fortunately, the Kumars are all hung up on the same programme, which is good for the family, with 30 out of 720 minutes of the day (that is, twelve hours, the daily quota of 'awake' time) being spent together.

The question is—would these precious thirty minutes spent watching television be called quality time? Yes of course, because this family harmony actually carries peace and calm to the child, seeping into his mind and psyche quite insidiously. Another use of this pastime is the opportunity for a value-based discussion. If you want to share some 'gyan' with your child, you can pick up on some point of interest from an episode of the soap, and use it to explain your point. But the child's receptivity quotient must be kept in mind. A preteen or teenager might resent it, and so may begin to avoid sitting with you at this time.

Quality time, or time spent parenting, does not mean that there has to be verbal or kinesthetic activity. Nonverbal cues are equally important, perhaps more so because they give the child a greater capability for independent thinking or introspection, both extremely important qualities for a successful life.

b) The value of family time as someone being there for you

An important aspect of family time is the notion of—'someone being there for you'—. This is a 360-degree feeling of comfort: someone to talk to, someone who helps you, does things for you, stands up for you, is concerned and interested to know how you are, someone to rely on, and who loves you despite all problems.

This phenomenon presents in two ways: one is the actual physical availability of the parent, and the other is the parent—who even though away at work—is always there for the child through all her times of need. Various studies by paediatric behavioural psychologists have evidenced that well-adjusted children, when asked whether they would like more time from their parents, unanimously answered 'NO'. So obviously, their needs can be fulfilled without the parents hovering around them all day. The assurance that their parents are there for them, whenever needed, is of much greater import.

(c) The value of having a say over one's time

Another important value for children is to be able to have a say over how they spend their time. Traditionally, the planning of household schedules, routines, and allocation of tasks were straightforward and uncomplicated—the prerogative of parents, as the caregivers of their children. But a schedule out of sync with the children's needs or wishes often creates much friction, and one of the worst nightmares for a parent is a frazzled child…such situations may also foster serious problems in the future.

On the other hand, when children perceive themselves as stakeholders in the creation of a busy family's time schedules, they utilise their time better. Allowing the child this privilege doesn't mean that the parents are spoiling her. On the contrary, such parents prepare their children to optimise a critical resource—the only constant entity in the universe—time. It can also become a very useful disciplining tool, as parents can use the withdrawal of this pleasant privilege as a punishment.

Conceptually, family time for children should not be seen only as time spent together, but also as time spent on their own.

(d) The value of time for having peace and quiet

There is something very interesting about parenting. In spite of loving their children unconditionally, parents harbour a very strong index of suspicion if they are out of sight inside the house. If a child is doing something on her own, they will keep popping in and disturbing her with silly questions.

It is important to understand that children value time on their own, for privacy and for peace and quiet. They like being able to make independent decisions about how their own time should be spent. Instead, parents fill the child's days and weekends with all kinds of activities like dance, dramatics, games, and other plans and commitments, over which the child may have very little say.

(e) The value of being able to plan one's own time

Closely related to the value of having time for peace and quiet is the quality of being able to plan one's time at home too. The tragedy is that things are not that simple. Children's daily time at home is shaped by everyday family routines, household organisation, and parental work patterns. It also depends on where the child lives. In townships or gated residential societies, there is a significant population of similar age group children, so they have an opportunity to have an independent social life with gated safety and security in addition. Smart parents give such opportunities to their children otherwise it becomes difficult for them to get used to planning their time.

If children are not encouraged to make independent decisions about how they manage their time at home and at school it does not equip them well to plan ahead for the short and long term. Children themselves perceived these skills and competencies as of crucial importance when they reached secondary school and had to fit in homework alongside more complex social commitments, family and other activities. One will find umpteen examples of children, who were high scorers in primary school lagging behind as they become more senior.

WHAT CAN A PARENT DO?

Here are some concise tips on how to put all these principles into practice when you are with your child:

- ✔ Do not lose patience
- ✔ Be spontaneous
- ✔ Let your inner child out to run free, it helps you as much as your child
- ✔ Limit discipline while making the effort to spend time together. It's no fun if all you're doing is scolding your child
- ✔ Don't get discouraged
- ✔ Use your imagination

The Jury Is Still Out: Quality Time vs Quantity Time   49

- ✔ Get creative; look around for new uses for everyday things
- ✔ Reflect on your own childhood frequently. Identify mistakes your parents made, and make an effort to avoid passing them on to the next several generations. (Every generation gets to make a whole set of new successes and/or mistakes.)

While following the above tips, you may find that you, too, are having a great time, with unbridled laughter or hysterical pandemonium, making you wonder if you are letting go of all controls. But this will not happen often; yet when it does, your children will cherish the memory for life. More commonplace is that you will be tired; but do try to lift yourself up; it just needs a little bit of effort. Don't forget all the extra work you do at your boss's command. Surely you can stretch yourself for your child too—you can delight her so, with a little fun activity or some companionship.

Remember that children grow fast, and will soon be on their way. Your boss may or may not recall that meeting you missed, but your children will never forget your not having attended the school annual function in which they had performed. Sometimes parents become very demanding and want the child to do the undoable. Always make sure that the activity you try is age-appropriate for your child. If it's too difficult, it's no fun.

One more issue parents face with their children is that

of the child's perception of favouritism as being bestowed on a particular sibling. It may be partly true because giving perfectly equal time to all is difficult, but one can spend it with each child individually. We have all grown up listening to various dictums and proverbs about the value of time, so there is no need to remind anyone to give their kids that ultimate gift.

Having talked about the child's point of view, it is also important to add here that parents should not compromise their own needs either. If you are at peace, and are doing things to the best of your abilities and circumstances, then your children would understand any limitations or shortcomings that may still crop up on your part. Share your work issues with them casually. This experiential learning will also help them in future when they pick up their own jobs. But be careful; share only the issues, not your discussions on personalities. That becomes gossip, which is an extremely harmful parental input.

Parenting is challenging because you are trying to meet another person's needs, one who is solely dependent on you. But again, that is also why it is so fulfilling! If done in a loving, considerate, and respectful manner, it is an incredible gift you are giving to your children and to the family, society, and community as well.

5
Crèche—the Dear Friend

Neha and Mayank Bajaj were feeling harassed. Even though only the first quarter of the year had gone by, they were precariously low on their leave reserve at work. Their daughter, Tia, was falling sick repeatedly—mostly fevers, sore throat and cough, or diarrhoea. A visit or two to the paediatrician would cure her, but the frequency of these episodes was killing. They knew that children fell sick more often than adults did; after all, they had brought up Vidur, their elder child too, but he had not fallen ill as regularly as Tia did.

Neha had quit her job when Vidur was born, and had continued the break for five years right up till Tia's birth. When she was two years old, Neha had taken up another job, thinking that a longer break would be detrimental to her career. Mulling over the problem, she shared her predicament with her cousin, Ila, who was in town for a business visit. Ila immediately asked her about Tia's routine, and insisted on visiting the crèche where she was cared for while Neha was away at office. Ila was very disturbed at what she saw and asked Neha to hunt for another crèche. They went around and found one, three kilometres further away in the opposite direction. Neha was very resistant to this unnecessarily increased commute. But her cousin, who was to quite an extent her best friend too, overpowered her refusal to go along with this change-over, and...hey presto, now three months have gone by without Tia visiting the doctor even once. Well what was the magic? Honestly, it lay in the change of the crèche.

BASIC REQUIREMENTS OF A CRÈCHE

Wikipedia very simply says 'crèche', 'creche', or 'cresch' may refer to a daycare centre—an organisation of adults who take care of children in place of their parents. This is an oversimplified definition because things are never this straightforward. So it is important to be vigilant about the facilities available in your child's crèche.

Staffing

Often it is seen that overenthusiastic and overconfident people in need of financial support, or of something to do—and who have some idle property—resort to opening a childcare centre. They may run it on their own, or with a minimal support staff. This is absolutely not practical because children need a large number of adults looking after them, if not the ideal ratio of one adult per child. So, do check if the number of assistants or helpers is sufficient. Also verify the standards of these employees, and of the facility's cleanliness. This is extremely important, as any laxity in these areas would lead to hygiene and sanitation issues, causing recurrent infections in your child, as was perhaps the case with Tia.

Space

It is difficult to maintain hygiene or cleanliness in congested areas. The crèche, or at least the rooms in which the children are kept, should have enough space to accommodate an appropriate number of children or cribs. Regardless of whether infants play and sleep in the same room, or in two separate rooms, the broad norms state that there shall be a minimum of 25 square feet of play space per child, plus a minimum of 30 square feet of sleeping space per child, with at least 2 feet between each crib.

Hygiene and sanitation

Cleanliness also means that toys used by the children be washed every day. This is only possible if they are made of high-grade plastic or polymer material. Soft toys do look cute, but are most unhygienic as they gather dust, fungus, and bacteria very quickly, and thus harbour and transfer infections. It is also important to enquire about bed linen, which should ideally be changed, and washed every day with a proper disinfectant, and dried in the sun if not in a drying machine. The cribs and mattresses should be placed outdoors by rotation, so that they are exposed to the sun and air at least twice in a week.

The crèche should be airy and exposed to sunlight too. Remember that any place that looks beautiful and organised does not necessarily mean that it is microbiologically sterile or clean. So, do ask about the cleaning schedule; how many times are the floors swept, and wet mopping done; are their multiple mops so that they can be sun-dried from time to time; what disinfectant is used in the mop water. Believe me, no good crèche organisers would shy away from answering these questions. If they follow good practices they would, rather, be proud to detail them out for you. Do not forget to check the cleanliness of the cooking area and also peep into the washrooms to appraise yourself of the sanitation.

Air-conditioning is critical in the case of toddlers and infants as their own temperature control system is not fully developed. If air-conditioning is not available, see to it that the crèche area is kept at an even temperature with the help of hot-air blowers or coolers. Extra care is required to ensure that the little ones are kept covered when necessary, as they tend to throw off coverings and wraps.

Location

In the morning hours, when both of you are rushing off to work, distances do matter. It would be ideal if the crèche were within two to three kilometres of your residence. Yet, 'if wishes were horses than beggars would ride', so try it the other way around—which is to bring your residence closer to the crèche. However, if you are living in your owned house, then this too, is a difficult or impractical proposition. If you can't manage to get closer to a good crèche then, to save your precious morning time, pack the baby's bags and do other preparations the night before, not forgetting anything she needs or craves for. Remembering baby's special requirements is paramount on the first or initial days.

In the case of an older child, you could have her pick out a special item to take along. A good facility should not have a problem with a blanket or toy from home that doesn't pose a hazard to others. It should also have space to store these belongings. If there is a good reason for not permitting any personal items, let your child pick out a picture—or better yet, help her make a small photo album or scrapbook—that can be looked at and shown around during the day. Your child may even come up with her own ideas for making the first day at the crèche more enjoyable.

Feeding issues

Usually a child is at the crèche for almost ten to twelve hours, so will consume perhaps one large and two small meals there, or multiple milk feeds. There are some crèches where, occasionally, you may be required to take your child's food along. If the crèche is providing the meals, which is a great comfort, then the smart parent needs to check out their cooking and serving practices. Try to see their weekly menu plan: are the items healthy and nutritious, is the crockery and cutlery perfectly cleaned and dried?

The hygiene factor becomes indispensable where drinking water is concerned. One may argue that we pack in sufficient water with our child, so we needn't bother about this issue. But do remember that your instructions to your child about drinking water from her own bottle only, would be followed more in breach than in toto. So keep reminding her about this and also be watchful of the drinking water provided at the crèche. Ideally, this should be pure potable water from a commercial water dispenser. If it is boiled and cooled water, then it should remain in the container in which it was boiled, as changing it may contaminate the water, leading to diarrhoea.

It is also crucial that a strict vigil be kept on the workers of the facility. Smriti was very happy with the first crèche, as there were no adjustment problems for her baby. Gradually, she realised that every time she went to pick up her child, he was groggy. On further enquiry she realised that the crèche workers were sedating the children to keep them sleeping all day. A horrified Smriti could not believe this terrible but true fact.

TRANSITION TO A NEW SETTING OR A NEW PERSON

Besides the physical issues of searching for, and deciding about the crèche, it is critical to address the psychological trauma encompassing such a change in the child's life. A daycare centre presents a whole set of potential adjustment problems: not only is the child with a new caregiver, but is also in an entirely new environment. It is much easier in the case of infants, as they settle down easily if their needs of hunger, sleep, and cleanliness are catered for. Depending upon your family circumstances, even an older child may have no trouble at all getting used to a new environment. The most difficult transition is with those older children, who have always been home with the parent as the primary caregiver.

Your job is to be supportive of your child, and not be pushy about playing with, or talking to, others if she is not yet comfortable doing so. It is vital to talk to your child about her feelings, if her age and understanding permits, but remember not to show your anxiety as that makes the child more apprehensive. Always be reassuring, explain why this new arrangement will be good (she will make friends, get to play, and so on), and above all, remain positive. Your child is likely to adopt your outlook. If you have a negative attitude about having to leave your child at the crèche, or over your return to work, chances are that she will perceive the predicament in a similar light. Although it has been seen that most children eventually make peace with the new order, be sure to ask during your interview, about how children with separation anxiety are handled. There are steps you, too, can take to facilitate the change in routine, and to ensure that your child is comfortable with the new setting.

The transition to the new crèche may go more smoothly if you introduce it to your child in stages. The more time she has to get used to the idea, prior to admission, the less painful the transition is likely to be. One of the best ways to put her at ease is to have her visit the facility, preferably more than once, for short spans. She can acquaint herself with the primary caregiver at the facility, as well as with the children who will be in her room. Some children may not interact at all, and it may also take some time before your own child is ready to participate, but that is all right.

Another way to ease this big change-over is to get your child on a wholesome sleep schedule several days, if not weeks, before the first day at the crèche. School-aged children typically need at least ten or eleven hours of sleep; toddlers and preschoolers even more. Determine how much time you and your child will require to unhurriedly prepare to leave each morning, and accordingly fix on a comfortable wake-up time for your child. Then count backwards to the number of sleep-hours she needs, and fix that as her bedtime. A regular time of sleep every night will help impart a sense of security during the transition phase.

∽

Try to spend a few minutes with her when putting her to bed. Sing, read a book, or just talk (or let her talk). Not only will these become cherished moments for both of you, but also, the dependability of the routine will help your child deal with feelings of uncertainty about going to a daycare centre.

∽

If your job permits, consider taking your child in for an hour or two only on the first day. Or, you could go into the facility an hour earlier than normal for the first few days, giving your child time to become accustomed to being there. If you do this, however, you will want to move her bedtime down by an hour as well, so that she still gets the necessary amount of sleep.

On the big day, when it is time to leave your child with the caregiver, reassure her that you *will* return at a specific time (such as after lunch, after naptime, or some other time that she will understand). Try, with the caregiver's help, to get her interested in an activity before you leave.

While departing, your child may show some distress; it is perfectly all right to give her a big hug, but it may also be necessary to be firm in explaining that you have to leave. If she remains resistant to your leaving, the caregiver should take over and allow you to go. Of course, you can, and should, contact the childcare provider at least once during the course of the day to see how your child is progressing.

A pattern of separation anxiety may repeat for more than a week or two. It is essential not to react negatively by a show of impatience or by being upset over your child's behaviour. Keep in touch with the crèche provider to see if your child remains agitated for a good part of the day, or if the tears dry up shortly after you leave. If the situation does not seem to resolve itself quickly, and the pattern continues beyond a couple of weeks, it will be necessary to examine the childcare setting to see if there is anything more than just separation anxiety.

In some cases, it is not your departure that is traumatic for your child, but simply arriving at the centre that triggers off the distress. Once a tantrum becomes a regular morning activity, it may be a difficult habit to break. If she acts out in your presence, but calms down once you leave, one possible answer might be to have someone else take her to the crèche for some days. Most parents are familiar with the phenomenon of their child being a little angel for everyone else but to them, so having a third party drop her off may help to curb the daily custom of throwing a fit at the daycare door.

Even if your child is adjusting fantastically to the new situation, your continued involvement in her activities there will help to keep her happy and secure at the centre. If the crèche is close to work, perhaps you can have lunch with her on a fixed day, or days, during the week. Even if it is hard to visit on a regular basis, visiting periodically with a special snack, or to read a book to the group, will reinforce your connection with your child even when apart.

If you have the facility of a maid taking care of your child at home, then too, a few things have to be borne in mind. Make sure that the maid is thoroughly apprised of the customs and procedures your child is familiar with, even to the minutest detail; for example, the temperature of milk she likes, or the amount of sugar in her milk.

If possible, have the maid come to your house for a few days while you are available at home, to guide her thorough a typical day with your child. Show her the locations of first aid materials, toys and games, cleaning supplies, cooking utensils, and other items that she may need. Explain to her when you would like meals to be served, and when the child should be put to nap. Go over the limits you would like enforced with regard to the use of televisions, phones, and computer games.

The better the maid's understanding of your rules and

expectations, the less confusion your child will experience with the new caregiver. All this may sound like a tough job, but is quite simple once you approach it with some preparation and logic.

6
Talk to Them, Don't Talk Down

The ability to communicate comes naturally to humans, but effective communication is an art that has to be learnt. While it is recommended that parents talk to their children as much as possible, many fall into the trap of talking *down* to their wards instead. Without realising it they sermonise, find faults, or even ridicule their children at every available opportunity. This is a sure-shot recipe to alienate them. Sooner or later they will either start avoiding you, or stop paying heed to your utterings.

Adults tend to underestimate children's ability to comprehend, and therefore, give oversimplified or even half-baked information. Instead of talking to them on an even keel, they try to brush aside their natural inquisitiveness. Repeatedly telling a child, 'you won't understand', 'you don't know', 'you can't do it', will not only deprive her of the opportunity to experiment and learn, it will also undermine her self-image.

Quantity as well as quality—both are important while communicating with children. If you don't communicate enough, you deprive the child of early auditory stimulation so imperative for speech development. If you talk in an irresponsible or base manner, you adversely affect the child's psyche. The worst offenders are those parents who talk very little and whenever they open their mouths it is to rebuke or say something negative about, or to, the child.

Lack of communication between parents and children is the bane of modern society. This is due mostly to time constraints, as busy parents try to meet deadlines on the job front. The more successful the parents, the more preoccupied they are with their careers and social engagements. So, naturally, despite wanting to spend time with their children, they are unable to do so. Children grow up so fast that parents who lose the opportunity of communicating with them while they are young, may never develop meaningful and warm relationships with them in later life.

Television is another important factor responsible for decreasing communications within the family. Many parents spend the entire evening watching TV, not bothering to interact with their children. Even if they do speak, it is to shut them up. Communication-deprived children suffer from delayed speech development, poor social adjustment, and lower IQs.

Good communication skills are the basis of any successful relationship, be it between husband and wife or parents and children. Unfortunately, many parents do not realise the relevance of proper interaction with their children. Some do, but still face problems while conversing. We hope the following examples will help to improve parent–child communications:

1. Khurana household

Mrs Neetu Khurana to son: 'You listen to me!'
Better approach: 'I want you to listen to me, and then you can speak and I will listen.'

A mistake that parents often make is that they talk but never listen. The child must know that when you finish talking, she will get a chance to speak as well. While communicating, the flow of ideas and thoughts should necessarily be two-ways, otherwise it becomes a lecture.

Remember: Communication = Talking + Listening. Try listening actively, and make encouraging gestures and sounds—nod your head, say 'yes', 'right', 'that's fine'.

2. Singh household

Mrs Aarti Singh to daughter: 'I don't believe you.'
Better approach: 'Promise not to lie, and I will believe you.'

Never begin the conversation with an accusation, because the child will end it with an immediate refusal.

If your opening line is: 'Why did you break the glass?' The most likely answer you will get is: 'I didn't.'

The better option would be to ask: 'How did the glass break?'

This will get the conversation going and you will receive a detailed account of the events leading to the breaking of the glass. You can use this opportunity to teach the child to be more responsible in future.

3. Tiwari household

Mr Arun Tiwari to son: 'You are an idiot of the highest order.'
Better approach: 'You need to apply yourself more.'

'Your room is worse than a pigsty.'
Better approach: 'Your room needs urgent cleaning.'

Parents must avoid flowery language and derogatory words when talking to their children. Reserve your eloquence for boardroom meetings, farewell parties, and obituaries. While communicating with children it is better to keep things straightforward and simple. This is especially important when dealing with a relatively young child, because more often than not, the child will either miss the point or misinterpret it. In the case of older children, use of sarcastic language can injure their pride and give them an inferiority complex.

4. Gupta household

Mr Shivendra Gupta to daughter: 'Come here immediately.'
Better approach: 'Let's get together in five minutes.'
'I want you home by seven positively.'
Better approach: 'Please be home between 7 and 7.30 p.m.'

There is no denying the power of spoken words; they are more potent than bullets. You can use them to attack, or protect, your child's personality. If children feel they are being attacked, they may clam up, or start arguing, or throw counter-accusations.

All these three situations interrupt the flow of communication, and may alienate the child. As a rule, communication will deteriorate if you use abusive language. Parents who constantly browbeat their child may succeed initially, but gradually the child will start paying back in the same coin. While handling children, a mild attitude and milder vocabulary usually produce the desired result.

5. Saxena household

Mr Rajeev Saxena teaching his son: 'Don't keep looking at the roof like a fool. The answer is not written there.'
Better approach: 'If you don't know the answer, take out your copy and read from it again.'

Try to recall when you were a kid—how much of the course did you remember yourself? It is human nature to forget one's own inadequacies and focus on others' faults. By such rantings you are not only damaging your child's confidence, you are undermining the entire parent–child relationship.

Agreed, our education system still retains the primitive rote-learning structure, but memorising the text without any understanding is not going to help in the long run. Entrance exams for most premier institutes are now becoming more and more analytical. The increasing emphasis on writing an SOP (Statement of Purpose), and GDPI (Group Discussion and Personal Interview), has changed the rules of the game during admissions, as well as in the job market.

FIVE ALTERNATE MODES OF COMMUNICATION

1. Non-verbal communication

A meaningful way of communicating with children is through eye contact and facial expressions. When you are socialising or in a setting where it is not possible to give verbal commands, you can show your approval or disapproval, by an encouraging or stern look, respectively.

The success of this form of communication depends upon prior conditioning of the child. Children are not expert face readers, so may not always be able to decipher the meaning behind your grim/happy/encouraging/discouraging look. Be prepared for this and don't get upset. Despite your best training, sometimes the child may avoid looking your way so as to act according to her own wishes. Don't take it too hard, children—after all—will be children.

2. Written communication

There are occasions when you need to communicate your feelings in writing. Parents and children should use this method more often, as written communication gives an opportunity to phrase one's thoughts more coherently. Notes praising your children for good behaviour, for helping in housework, or for doing well in studies, are great morale boosters for them. Parents can pleasantly surprise their children by slipping a message into their pencil box or notebook, saying that they love them very much, or are proud of them.

Notes can also be used to register a complaint without creating a scene. When you expect a showdown or want to avoid an unnecessary argument, written notes are the best way to express your displeasure.

3. Demonstrative communication

While lecturing or running down a child, parents never fall short of adjectives and similes. But when it comes to communicating feelings of love and caring, many are found wanting. Often, our first real proof of parental love is when we fall sick. This transmits the message that illness, injury, and other adverse situations are a prerequisite for receiving love and care. Parents must ensure that children do not get such a distorted picture of the parent–child relationship. The line: 'If you love somebody, show it', may sound clichéd but it, nevertheless, holds true for innumerable parents. So try to demonstrate your love, show you care, and express your feelings.

Demonstrative communication can be verbal or physical. Some verbal statements you can use are:

- 'I am really proud to have a son/daughter like you.'
- 'If I scold you it doesn't mean that I don't love you.'
- 'I am lucky to have such a conscientious/dependable/meticulous child like you.'

Don't assume your child knows that you feel this way; communicate it to her in your own words.

Physical demonstration of feelings plays a major role in the development of a warm and loving parent–child relationship. Children who have plenty of emotional and physical contact with their parents find it easier to give and receive love. Never miss an opportunity to hug, kiss, or cuddle your child. If you don't give love today, your child will not learn to receive it tomorrow—neither from you, nor from anyone else. It has been observed that such children are non-demonstrative themselves, and may have unproductive relationships in later life.

4. Supportive communication

For proper expression of emotions, and to sustain communications, a good vocabulary is a must. Children may face problems while communicating because they lack experience in labelling their feelings. When they fail to find appropriate words, and are unable to correctly verbalise their emotions, they are likely to become frustrated. This can cause behavioural problems and destructive tendencies. Sometimes, in haste, they may choose the wrong words and offend their parents, so their conversations may deteriorate into an argument.

Parents must help their children to correctly label a feeling or emotion. Here are some examples, which can be used to assist the child:

- 'I get the feeling from your behaviour that you are trying to say _ _ _ _.'
- 'While you sound angry, it is actually your frustration over _ _ _ _.'
- 'I guess you want to communicate that _ _ _ _.'

5. Anticipatory communication

A good parent can anticipate the child's mood and reaction to a situation. If you are observant enough you can see some non-verbal response: a dull look, a deadpan face, brimming eyes, or intense denial. If you can latch on to these expressions you will have instant access to the child's emotional turmoil. The child will also have an easier time communicating with you because she can sense your involvement and concern. Parents who are good at anticipatory communication have a very good chance of identifying and dealing with their child's problems.

7
Punishment Doesn't Pay

Parents have to educate their children, instil values, and teach proper behaviour. This is not an easy task, and at times their patience is tested to the limits. The stress and strain of modern living takes a heavy toll on parents who are perpetually on the verge of blowing their fuses. That last act of indiscretion on the part of their child brings about a regrettable explosion. When the realities and disappointments of parenting shatter the dreams of ideal parenthood, anxiety and guilt are the result.

The triggers are many and varied, but stress and exhaustion come high on the list. Some parents seem to believe that to make their children tough, they need to be punished. Their argument is: 'We don't want our children to be fragile flowers who will wilt the moment the heat is turned on.' Mrs Usha Saxena, a working mother, says: 'I have resorted to an occasional slap to discipline my children. This happened when I had an unusually long list of things to squeeze into an already crowded schedule, and was very tired. I have also lost my temper when my children encroached upon the last vestiges of my personal time and space.'

Physical punishment contravenes all norms of good parenting, and those who resort to it agree that it doesn't even work. Regular physical punishment also gradually loses its impact, and may either induce stubborn behaviour or rebellion. Punishment damages parent–child relationships irreversibly, and what could have been a lifelong bond of love and warmth, is lost on the altar of uncontrolled anger. It will serve parents better to remember Mark Twain's words, 'When angry, count four; when very angry, swear'.

Punishing the child provokes a conflict in the minds of most parents. The turmoil of simultaneously loving and hating the child becomes difficult for them to handle. The dilemma of whether to punish or not has no simple solution. Parents feel guilty if they punish the child, and frustrated when they suppress the urge. Most parents don't punish their children because they think it is the best option, but because they feel drained, dominated, exploited, criticised, and even humiliated.

A child doesn't understand the difference between 'hitting' and 'hating', and may view corporal punishment by a parent as hate and dislike for her. She is not in a position to reason that your punitive action is merely a manifestation of temporary anguish, and that in reality you do still love her a lot.

The *Oxford Dictionary of Current English* describes 'Discipline' as 'training or way of life aimed at self-control and conformity'. Disciplining children is no mean job. When you try to discipline your child, you are dealing with an extremely versatile and sensitive brain, capable of reasoning and decision-making. So the onus is on you to be equally reasonable, imaginative, and compassionate. Think about this: hitting a child when she is out of control shows that you, too, have lost it. As an adult, you are expected to manage your emotions better, certainly more so than a young, inexperienced child!

Most parents are also confused as to what constitutes extremes of strictness or leniency. Too strict an approach is likely to lead to confrontation. Too lenient an attitude is commensurate with disobedience, disregard, and even delinquency. No one would advocate physical punishment for teaching discipline, but an occasional ear-twisting must be differentiated from habitual abuse.

The three cardinal rules for effective disciplining are:

- Be realistic
- Be consistent
- Be supportive

TEACH DISCIPLINE—AVOID PUNISHMENT

Evolve a suitable disciplinary model for your family and stick to it if you want to avoid punishing your child. Here are some tips to accomplish this basic task.

1. Have guidelines and implement them consistently

Having a set of guidelines for proper behaviour is the first step in the direction of controlling impropriety. If children are bound by well-defined limits, they are likely to remain within them. Laxity in implementing set rules could result in unnecessary tension and frequent inappropriate behaviour. It is important that correct behaviour is rewarded and negative behaviour punished, but more important is the consistency of such rewards and punishments. Uniformity of discipline helps the child in developing a frame of reference, which leads to a fair degree of homogeny in her behavioural pattern.

2. The KISS concept

KISS stands for—Keep It Straight and Simple. This concept not only holds true for teaching discipline, it is valid in every aspect of life. While disciplining your child, it is better to keep things simple, to speak honestly, and without melodrama. If you tell her: 'You have made me very angry', it will have a more positive impact than calling her a 'horrible brat' or 'an idiot'. Using impractical and complex commands while awarding punishment, also, never results in any behavioural improvement.

If you do decide to punish the child, avoid physical punishment at all costs. For example, asking the child to catch hold of her ears and stand atop a table will become useless and problematic if she falls and hurts herself. You may even have to rush around to dress her wound if she starts bleeding.

3. Avoid unnecessary confrontation

As in life, so in parenting—a confrontationist attitude can land you in trouble, while an ability to remain calm and find amicable solutions can take you places. If your child is upset, angry, or frustrated, avoid getting entangled in her foul mood. Refrain from picking up an unnecessary argument, as it may lead to an entirely avoidable situation, forcing you to take much harsher measures than you normally would.

One night when Yashdeep returned home very late, his father Mr Harish Goyal, blew his fuse. 'Do you realise what time it is?' he shouted, pointing at the wall clock showing the time as 10.15 p.m. 'Your exams are just around the corner and you are loitering with your good-for-nothing friends!'

Yashdeep didn't reply and started to climb the stairs to go up to his room on the first floor.

'I am talking to you! Don't you even have the courtesy to reply to your father?' Mr Goyal barked.

'I was at Ankit's place. We were studying together for the exams,' snapped Yashdeep.

'Liar, do you think I am a fool? Where are your books?' Mr Goyal moved towards Yashdeep menacingly.

'I was studying with Ankit,' said Yashdeep, getting visibly upset and frustrated.

'You must be the first student who studies without books,' shouted Mr Goyal. 'I *know* you had gone to the mall with those "awara" friends of yours.'

'Think whatever you want, I am not bothered,' replied Yashdeep in an angry tone.

Mr Goyal went wild with rage and delivered a resounding slap on Yashdeep's face. The impact made Yashdeep lose his balance and he fell down the stairs, sustaining a cut on his chin. Mrs Goyal came rushing out of the bedroom and on seeing Yashdeep's wound, began reprimanding her husband.

This is how the mishandling of a minor, day-to-day situation, can turn into a major, ugly confrontation.

Let's now look at an alternate and more rational approach to tackle this incident.

One night when Yashdeep returned home very late, his father Mr Goyal said, 'Yash, come wash your hands quickly. Your mom and I have been waiting to have dinner with you.'

'In a minute, Dad,' replied Yashdeep, looking at the wall clock guiltily.

'Your exams are just around the corner, I hope you are studying hard,' spoke Mr Goyal, looking pointedly at Yashdeep.

'Yes, Dad, I had gone to Ankit's house to study maths. You know he is very good at maths. After some time we got bored and went off to the mall for ice cream.' Yashdeep took a chapati from the casserole as his mother served him potato curry.

'So that's why you became late today,' said Mr Goyal without a trace of accusation in his voice. 'But where are your books?'

'I left them at Ankit's place because I intend to study with him again tomorrow.' Yashdeep took another chapati and placed it on his plate. 'And Dad, tomorrow onwards I don't intend to go to the mall till the exams are over.'

'That's a good boy,' smiled Mr Goyal, patting Yashdeep's back.

More or less the same questions and concerns are raised in both sets of conversations. The abrupt, accusatory, and confrontationist attitude in the former leads to an extremely unsavoury situation, while the mild, understanding, and positive approach of the latter diffuses a potentially volatile scenario.

4. Double fault

When Praveer was young, he would often enter the drawing room and, without greeting the guests, pick up whatever he wanted to eat from the centre-table, make funny faces, and run away to play outside. His parents never scolded him for his misdemeanours, and sometimes they, and even the guests, found his antics cute. With time, this behaviour got ingrained, and he developed a devil-may-care attitude towards others and their feelings.

Much later, when Praveer was in Class IX at school, this insensitivity got him into serious trouble. One evening, he returned home from the playground to find his father having tea with some guests. As was his habit, without acknowledging their presence or wishing them, he dropped his cricket bat on the floor, picked up some biscuits from a plate, and pushed off to his room.

His father became furious, and after the guests had left, barged into Praveer's room shouting, declaring him to be an uncouth, uncivilised boy sans any manners. In between, he landed several blows on Praveer's body. As he bellowed on and on, Praveer sank down on the bed sobbing, an uncomprehending expression on his bewildered face.

Childhood is the age for discipline, and adolescence the time to develop a friendship with your child. So at both stages, the fault lay with the parents, but the child got the blame.

The first mistake parents often make is not teaching discipline at the right age. When the child is very young, they feel it is too early for her to be taught about right or wrong behaviour, saying there is sufficient time for that later. The child grows up not even knowing that she is doing anything wrong, because no one has ever told her so!

After this, the parents commit the second mistake by unexpectedly imposing a stern discipline on their totally unprepared teenaged child. All of a sudden, they expect her to be the epitome of exemplary behaviour, to don a persona for which she has not been trained at all.

The good habits they didn't much bother to inculcate earlier, and the manners they didn't sufficiently emphasise upon, now suddenly become pivotal for them, much to the child's chagrin.

5. Rewards and punishment

Rewards: Who doesn't want recognition for good work or a good deed? Children, especially, need a pat on the back for conforming to prescribed norms of behaviour. Punishment only acts as a deterrent, it tells the child what not to do, but rewards teach accepted and expected behaviour. They also reinforce correct behaviour, and are a must if long-term behavioural changes are desired.

Parents may feel that there is no need to reward a child for doing what is expected. But they must realise that children have only a vague notion of what is appropriate and what isn't. In doing what is right, the child is making a special effort, and this needs to be appreciated. Rewarding your child for brushing her teeth at night, without being told to do so, reinforces the continuation of the habit. Rewards can be in any of the following forms:

- Monetary
- Verbal praise
- Written notes of thanks
- Extra time to play or watch TV
- A small gift
- A delayed bedtime
- A spontaneous hug

Punishment: Choosing an appropriate punishment for inappropriate behaviour is definitely more difficult than giving rewards. Parents should avoid harsh and impracticable punishments; for example, 'no picnics or eating out till you improve your ranks.' This may dishearten the child and can cause rebellion. Even worse, you will have to sit at home on weekends to cook and feed your convict.

Asking the child to stand in a corner for ten minutes can be controlled, but making him stand for a full sixty minutes may be difficult to implement. Some urgent work may require your immediate attention and the child may simply vanish from the scene. Leaving a punishment incomplete will not have the desired effect; on the contrary, it can make the child more obstinate and difficult to manage.

Never trade a punishment for a reward on the DSE (Disciplinary Stock Exchange). In other words, the consequence for a misdeed should never be nullified by a reward for good behaviour; both must be dealt with separately. What do you do if your child completes her homework but leaves the study table in a mess? Praise the child for finishing her assignment, but at the same time reprimand her for not cleaning the table. It would be wrong to say: 'Okay, as you have done your homework, it more than makes up for leaving your table in a mess.' If you begin trading in discipline, your child is bound to learn the trade quickly. She will prove to be an astute businessman picking up bargain deals, but getting undisciplined in the bargain.

6. Put up a united front

While disciplining their child, parents must put up a united front. If one parent disagrees with the other's tactics, it should be discussed at a private moment. Open disagreement regarding a disciplinary action not only confuses the child, but also makes her bitter towards the seemingly unjust parent. As described earlier, if you have clear guidelines for acceptable/unacceptable behaviour, this situation need not arise.

Never ever shift the responsibility of disciplining on to your spouse. 'Wait until your father comes home', is a common refrain of many mothers. This must be avoided at all costs, as it gives a negative message to the child. It implies that you are incapable of controlling the situation, which can make the child more belligerent. By relinquishing disciplinary powers to your husband, you place him in an unenviable position. His personality acquires demonic proportions, and he is forced to shout whenever he meets the children.

Disciplining is a physically and mentally draining job. Even before you finish patting yourself for successfully managing a tricky situation, a fresh crisis arises. You can run out of ideas and techniques to deal with your children's indiscipline, and your frustration levels may escalate. In such circumstances, delay dealing with children immediately. Send them to their room saying that you will deal with them later. That time gap will allow you to regain your control and recoup your energy. It also reduces impractical consequences, as it allows for a different perspective than that viewed at the height of your anger.

Sometimes, one parent chooses to hide the child's indiscipline from the other parent. This may be justified when it is done to protect the child from a parent who is known to be violent and abusive. Such protection can salvage the child's personality from total devastation. However, concealing inappropriate behaviour actually increases the child's anxiety level and gives the message that the other parent is to be feared. The child starts fantasising a fatal consequence should the feared parent discover her inappropriate behaviour. In most cases it is better for the child to face the music from both speakers—one producing bass, the other treble.

7. Temper tantrums

If a child is upset or angry, and speaks out her mind without being abusive or destructive, let her do so. Vocalisation of frustration and anger reduces the child's tension, and must be tolerated by parents. However, screaming and cursing should not be permitted, especially if it is directed at the parents. Limits must be set, and the child should be taught appropriate ways of venting her feelings. Allowing the child to get away with verbal abuse can be very damaging for her in the long run.

Tackling temper tantrums requires much patience, some firmness, and a bit of foresight. Children have a knack of choosing the most inopportune place and time for throwing a tantrum, such as at a relative's place, a crowded market, an ice-cream parlour, and so on. If the scene is being enacted at home, be patient and let the child calm down. You have to be firm and in control, if it occurs at a relative's or a friend's place. Finally, you must have the sense to avoid toyshops and ice-cream parlours when your child accompanies you to the market.

Don'ts in Dealing with Temper Tantrums

- Don't allow the child to have an audience for displaying her histrionics; remove her to a room or any other isolated area.

> - Don't try to reason with her when she is in this state.
> - Don't hesitate to tell her that there will be a consequence later for her bad behaviour.
> - Don't delay rewarding her if she checks or aborts a tantrum spontaneously to communicate with you.

8. Family time

The importance of family time, when all the members sit together, cannot be over-emphasized. Whether over evening meals, or while having tea/coffee/milk, these occasions bind the family together and provide a platform for sharing achievements, venting frustrations, and sharing good advice. Parents can use this time to subtly guide their wards, and mould them towards functioning successfully in society.

Evening meals can also be used to facilitate communication between warring parties. But, beware! Better communication is not synonymous with 'sermonising'. Avoid lecturing your child at the dining table; instead listen to her point of view.

'A family that eats together stays together'. We think nothing can be truer than this famous proverb.

Other wonderful and memorable family occasions include playing a game together—indoors or out, enjoying a picnic, or any other interactive family pastime.

8
Parent–Teacher Meeting— Making the Most of It

Every child begins life within a particular family. The child is raised with certain traditions and values. These, in spite of being socially uniform, are unique to each family. When a child goes to school she meets diverse individuals. Out of these, the most powerful is the teacher with a commanding role as guide, mentor, and counsellor. Not only do parents expect the teacher to play all these roles effectively, but the pupils too, look up to them for these needs.

Back in time, teachers were placed on a pedestal, but today, that pedestal seems to be crumbling. Even so, in comparison to the parents, a child would still hold at least one or two teachers at a level of eminence. It is important to keep in mind that the learning and discipline a school-going child acquires, also requires frequent collaborative communications between parents and teachers. Out of the sixteen waking hours, almost seven to eight, (or 40–50 per cent) are spent in school. Needless to say that—studies apart—all the inputs at school are of major significance. It becomes doubly important when both parents are out working, because there is a limit on the time they can give their child. In such a situation, the teacher can provide a strong support system for them.

OH NO! THE PARENT–TEACHER MEETING...

It was the third Thursday of the month, in the second quarter of the academic year, and as usual, Abeer and Trisha were trying to push each other to attend the parent–teacher meeting (PTM) at school the next day. Since Trisha had gone to the previous, first PTM of the academic year, she told Abeer that she would not go the next time. 'Such a waste of two hours, yaar; had to unnecessarily take half-day chhutti and obligation of my project leader.' According to her, she had met with a number of her child's teachers, but the music teacher had nothing to say to her, nor had the language teacher, or even the class teacher. Trisha, herself, had remained quiet. In fact she'd thought she had more to say to her grandmother's cousin, whom she had met on the way to school that day. She honestly believed that only her child could give her the full picture of her own educational progress.

Is Trisha right about parent–teacher meetings being a waste of time? Well actually, Trisha did not know what questions to ask, and hence the meeting became a silent and empty event for her.

WHAT IS A PARENT–TEACHER MEETING?

A parent-teacher meeting is actually a time for the sharing of thoughts, and the methods of teaching, keeping the welfare of the child at the centre. It is a building block for a two-way relationship between parents and teachers. When handled correctly, these meetings provide an opportunity for the teacher to explain the child's progress in studies, and personality traits and development, to the parents. If you really wish to gauge the abilities of a teacher then, in the first meeting itself, you can gain an understanding of the teacher's personality and skills.

A good teacher would have gathered her thoughts about your child's personality traits, intellect, proficiencies, and other important aspects, and would know of the specific competencies and knowledge to be imparted to her. Yes, it is true that your first response would be that every child has to complete the same course and syllabus as defined for that class. But a good teacher would, in spite of these restrictions, snip off unnecessary things in order to optimise the course for the child. Hence identifying even one or two such teachers, and interacting with them, would be immensely beneficial for your child.

HOW TO GO ABOUT A PTM

- The preparation has to begin much before the actual PTM.
- It is always helpful to have a folder about your child on your laptop/tab/diary/notebook. In this, you should record your questions and observations about your child, or the school, or any other related issues. But do go through it before the meeting; don't refer to it in front of the teacher who may consider you hyper or overaggressive.
- Be there on time, but ready to wait, because parents before you may have exceeded their meeting time slots. Hence, do not consider unpunctuality as the teacher's fault.
- It is useful to open the conversation by asking, very briefly, about the proposed or planned activities of the school, or the particular class. This usually makes the teacher less apprehensive and more eager to share. Some parents have a tendency to start accusing the school, or the teacher, as soon as they take their seat. Inadvertently, this pushes the teacher into a corner, and puts even the best on their guard.
- Then you can share information about your family or child such as may have a bearing on her behaviour or mood at school; for example, a new baby sibling, the loss of a grandparent, or a parent's relocation to another town. Children find it difficult to understand or share

their emotions thus generated, but their behaviour is definitely impacted. Teachers, who are unaware of such events in the life of their student, will lack the appropriate sensitivity in handling the child.
- The next thing to do is to ask about your child's progress. You should have also taken, beforehand, your child's own opinion on this matter. Generally, you will find that the child has some discontent or grudge against the teacher. Try to probe those issues with the teacher, but do remember that it should be tackled very tactfully.
- You can request to see your child's classwork (if not made available to you routinely), as she would have handled this more-or-less independently, reflecting her own capabilities. You should also ask, or try to gauge, the teacher's expectations of your child, and what you can do at home to strengthen them.
- The teacher's time is at a premium, so if your meeting has been lengthy with issues still remaining, then perhaps you can seek a future appointment with the teacher, at a mutually convenient date and time.
- Later, you must introspect about the issues covered at the meeting. First get your thoughts and observations in order, and then discuss your conclusions with your child. Take care not to be judgmental, because she is already apprehensive about you and the teachers having met. She believes that it was a cribbing session between the two, the butt being herself!

Try to read between the lines, because with experience and training, teachers tend to speak a diplomatic language. When talking about the apples of our eyes, teachers have to tread very, very carefully. They take care to express themselves in terms that are professional, constructive, and kind. So, when a preschool teacher says: 'Aarav is still developing his ability to relate to other children,' she really means: 'Aarav is mean.' The reason the teacher doesn't actually say that is because you may pick up a fight or think of changing the school.

A good teacher understands many telltale signs too: if she sees one child hit another, she can figure out what the child is trying to accomplish. She starts thinking of teaching the child a different way to get what she wants. Half the time when kids appear to be anti-social, they are actually trying to be friendly, but don't know how. So, perhaps what is needed is more patience and desire to peer into, and understand, tiny minds. For this, both the teacher and parent have to cooperate with each other.

DO NOT LET THE FEAR FACTOR OVERTAKE YOU

Frequently, it has been found that parents are not able to take full advantage of PTMs because of their own fears or complexes. These could be:

- *Fear of divulging family conflicts or secrets, even though they may be impinging on the child's behaviour or performance at school*

Please do not forget that hiding any kind of child abuse, sexual or otherwise, would disallow proper handling at this critical stage. If not attended to now, it would leave a permanent scar on the child's psyche, leading to future unhappiness and complications. Every school has a counsellor, so take advantage of this facility.

- *Anxiety over your child's possible failure*

If you feel this way, then do remember—no one is born a failure. Everyone can achieve something, even those with disabilities. You just need to match their special talent with an appropriate vocation. Albert Einstein said 'Everybody is a genius. But if you judge a fish by its ability to climb a tree, it will live its whole life believing that it is stupid.'

- *Guilt over lack of parenting skills*

Oh, do not dig yourself into a hole of blame, shame, and guilt. Whatever your child is doing wrong is not because of any lack of your parenting skills. In fact, no one is expected to know everything about being a parent—it's a skill one has to learn, just like any other. The bottom line is that feeling blamed and guilty prevents us from taking action. It keeps us stuck and defeated; it becomes the smudgy lens through which we see things, rather than a clear vision focusing on behavioural change. Do not withdraw or pull away. Discuss the situation with the school counsellor. While there's no one 'right way' of parenting, there *are* always better or more effective ways to handle your child's errant behaviour.

- *Do not be abashed or reluctant to interfere in the teacher's work*

All teachers need strategies to determine the pace and progress of their students' learning. This information provides them with the basis for making decisions, planning instructional activities and experiences, and distinguishing between effective and ineffective procedures. Constructive monitoring helps teachers take ownership of the teaching–learning process and enables them to implement new methods to foster students' educational growth. This can happen satisfactorily only when augmented with parental feedback.

- *Parents should know that they matter in the scheme of things*

Many parents, consciously or subconsciously, believe that they wouldn't know how to add value in school: they doubt the degree of their ability to make a difference. Although people can learn new roles and skills, their desire and capacity for effective involvement will be enhanced or limited, by their own beliefs, barriers, or opportunities in connection with, for example, language, or practical skills in understanding and negotiating the school system.

- *Do not let your bad experiences overshadow your child's future*

The parents' negative experiences as students have a strong influence in their interactions during parent–teacher meetings. But remember, you can't run away, or be an ostrich and hide. You have to fight your demons for the sake of your child. Once you stand up to your inhibitions you can definitely overcome them.

9
Hone Your Child's Talent

EVERY CHILD IS GIFTED

Although this point appears at the top, it is the bottom line of this chapter. All children have immense potentialities, and several hidden talents. Opportunities, or the lack of them, can either make or mar a child's future prospects. It is the responsibility of the parents to recognise and nurture their child's talent. As mentioned earlier, engineer, doctor, or teacher—the only three choices that existed some years back—have given way to not less than a hundred viable and well-paid career options. These are so wide and varied that it is quite possible that a child will turn his talent into a profitable career.

Devang was fortunate to be studying in a school where equal weightage was given to co-curricular activities as to the academics. The school had several hobby sections like 'woodwork, 'metalwork', 'papermaking', 'automobile work' and other skills. With the help of his carpentry instructor, Devang accomplished the crafting of a set of wooden clothes hangers and a magazine stand. His father was extremely impressed by the good workmanship and finish of the articles. At home, Devang enjoyed making useful objects with the help of do-it-yourself kits available at the nearby supermarket.

After completing school, Devang was a bit confused about the various career options available to him. One evening after dinner, his father and mother sat down with him to discuss the choices. They talked about engineering and architecture, but finally the discussion veered around to designing. Devang was excited by the prospect of becoming a product designer. Through sheer hard work, he was selected for admission into a premier design college, where he excelled, ranking amongst the top three during the entire course. He worked in a leading design house for two years, but finally quit and set up his own furniture showroom. Today, his business venture is flourishing; he has opened a second outlet, and his firm is known for the most innovative and modern furniture in town.

Undoubtedly, Devang worked hard for the success he attained. But can his parents' role in identifying his talent be overlooked? They are both doctors, yet they didn't coerce him into entering their profession. Instead, they helped nurture his designing skills, and facilitated his career choice. We don't know whether we can call them smart parents or not, but we can certainly declare them to be involved and conscientious.

If your child's school doesn't offer extra-curricular activities, try to take that responsibility upon yourself. Let teachers teach; meanwhile you can augment the child's education outside of school, by introducing him to varied activities. New interests and pursuits have the capacity to bring alive, and excite, our sleeping brain cells. They also act as safety valves and help in releasing pent-up stresses. The sense of achievement associated with developing new skills, and honing existing talents gives us happiness and fulfilment. It motivates us to pursue and attain our goals successfully.

∼

Ritika was always interested in books. Even as a little preschool child, she would pick one up, sit between her parents and mimic them read. By the time she was eight, she was through with Enid Blyton, at ten she had finished the Harry Potter series and had moved onto more serious stuff.

Her parents were themselves voracious readers, and wrote for various newspapers and magazines. They noticed her craving for the written word, and took her to book fairs that came to the town from time to time. For this family, purchasing of books was the one thing for which there were no budgetary limits. Soon Ritika had a mini library of her own. She began to write poems and short stories, some of which got published in children's magazines.

She passed her Class X exams with flying colours. During her summer vacation, her father sent her to London (to his younger brother) to attend an eight-week creative writing course. After her return she wrote a novella based on her school experiences. Although it didn't create any waves, it gave her the confidence to attempt more serious subjects later.

After completing her graduation, Ritika did her MA in English literature. All the while, she kept contributing articles to various newspapers and magazines. She published her first novel when she was twenty-six. Today at thirty-five, with three bestselling books behind her, Ritika is a name to reckon with in literary circles.

Of course Ritika's success is largely due to her own aptitude and attitude. No one can teach creativity, but optimal nurturing can certainly bring it to the fore. The role of her parents in identifying, supporting, and polishing her talent must be appreciated and applauded.

Human creativity is at its peak during adolescence. Parents must try to assess the child's potential and special interests, to the best of their ability. Adolescent imagination, inquisitiveness, and exuberance need to be directed into constructive endeavours. If this bountiful energy is left underutilised it may go waste, or might get misdirected into unwanted and unlawful activities.

Pulkit was a robust, tall lad who often got into scuffles with his classmates. Sometimes the mistake was his, but on several occasions, others were at fault. Such was his reputation that teachers invariably presumed him to be the culprit, even when he wasn't. It was not that he was bad at studies, but somehow his heart was not in academic pursuits.

His father, a cricket enthusiast who had played as an opening batsman for his college, was observing all this from the sidelines. He knew Pulkit was good at sports, winning the 100-metre race at school every time. This gave his father the idea to motivate Pulkit to join the nearby cricket academy to try his hand at fast bowling.

The local coach was impressed by Pulkit's speed and natural outswing. For the first time, Pulkit was enjoying what he was doing. Very shortly, he was selected for the district team. As luck would have it, the state cricket team was in town to play a Ranji Trophy match, and he was invited to bowl during net-practice. He bowled with fire, and all the established batsmen found him too hot to handle! Next year he joined the state Ranji team, and was also picked up by a prominent IPL franchisee. When Pulkit took two wickets, and hit the winning boundary in his very first IPL match, not only his parents and neighbourhood, but also the entire city was ecstatic.

There are many Pulkits who have made it big with proper guidance and support. The parents have a crucial role to play in the timely identification of the child's unique capability. If they follow it up with prompt interventions, the sky is the limit for their child. On the other hand, neglect or delay in recognising and reinforcing a child's inherent competence, will prevent her from achieving her optimal potential.

~

Children are naturally curious, and when their queries are solved by real-life experiences, as against textbook knowledge alone, they are better able to understand and retain the learnings. A photograph of the Red Fort or Taj Mahal can never have the same impact as seeing the real thing. It's not only about historical monuments; a widely travelled child has a broader area of interest and a greater pool of knowledge. There is so much to explore in and around every city: rivers, lakes, forests, and hills. There are ancient buildings and museums to be visited; and factories, dams, and power stations to learn from.

Aahna's parents believed that travel is the best way to educate a child. They took her on frequent outdoor trips and various sightseeing tours. Aahna learnt from these outings what no classroom could ever teach her. She started to enjoy these trips, and began participating in their planning. With a little guidance from her parents, she soon started to chalk out the entire programme herself, including the travel and hotel arrangements. When she was in Class XII, she—with some help from her father—organised a family reunion at Mount Abu, in which almost thirty members from both sides, maternal and paternal, came together.

After obtaining a degree in hotel management, Aahna worked for a while in the hospitality industry. In her free time, she would be found hovering around the desk of an in-house travel agency. Soon she switched jobs and started to work at the head office of that agency. Today, after five years, she owns a travel agency of her own and caters to both—niche travelers going to exotic destinations, as well as group travellers visiting Kullu–Manali and Nainital.

The urge to travel and visit new places, inculcated by her parents, only became stronger with time. Aahna not only loved to travel and see new places but also enjoyed planning the trips for her customers, and her unbridled enthusiasm for tourism endeared her to her clients. It is no surprise that her agency has become hugely popular, and she is extremely successful.

∼

Whether it was a neighbourhood cultural activity, a school function, or any other competition, **Sankalp's** parents consistently motivated him to participate in them. With opportunities galore, Sankalp gradually became stage savvy, and this confidence automatically followed him into other areas as well. With changing times, the spectrum of career options has changed and widened exponentially, including for people with interests like Sankalp. So, he did some fashion modelling assignments during his graduation, and then diversified into television. Today, he hosts a popular chat show on TV besides being an established model.

The stage is like a miniature-art form, that prepares the child to paint successfully on the canvas of life. It provides opportunities to demonstrate various latent talents and skills. Success on the stage boosts the self-image and allows the child to face the world with assurance. Whether it's an oral exam or a job interview, the candidate who walks in confidently and speaks with conviction, usually gets through. Individuals who were active onstage during their formative years succeeded in conventional jobs as well. Their ability to speak eloquently, and the confidence acquired while facing large gatherings comes in handy in all work situations.

Parents should motivate their children to participate in stage activities from early childhood. If not, the diffident ones will succumb to the well-known phenomenon of stage fright. Many capable and highly intelligent persons find themselves totally helpless when asked to step up on the stage. The inability to face an audience, and to express one's thoughts and views with ease, remains a major handicap in many people's lives.

Although parents have an important role to play in

honing their child's talent, they should not hesitate to bring in an expert when they feel the need for it. If your child shows an aptitude for painting and you can't draw a mango, you should enrol him in a class run by a professional. The same is true for other activities like music, dance, photography, and various indoor and outdoor games. The crux of the matter is that, whatever your child's talent, you must be passionate about nurturing it.

10
The Concept of Uniqueness

All children have different needs. Even with twins, one child will have to be fed first—her needs will take priority over the other who is more patient and thus has to wait. Later, the impatient one may have strong likes and dislikes while the other continues to be happy with whatever she gets. This is an undesirable state because the demanding child has her wishes fulfilled while the other one is left behind. Parents must cater to the needs of the reticent child so that she doesn't in any way feel less cared for.

One child will express her views, thoughts, and preferences freely; the other may be introverted and quiet. At mealtimes, or other similar occasions, parents should create opportunities and persuade the quiet one to speak. They can ask direct questions and may even have to instruct the talkative one to simply shut up.

Parents face an eternal dilemma at the dining table

because usually what one child likes the other hates. Bhindi (ladies' fingers) is probably the only vegetable uniformly liked by all children. But, even here, our elder daughter likes them split lengthwise while the younger one must have them chopped small. If both your children are equally doughty and evenly matched in physique, you will have a harrowing time deciding on the menu. But then it was your very own decision to have two children!

Even very young babies manifest uniqueness in response. Some of them startle at the slightest sound, or cry if bright light hits their faces; others are seemingly insensitive to such stimuli. This tendency to react differently to similar triggers is carried forward from infancy to adulthood, explaining why similar conditions evoke varying reactions in different individuals.

The best way to bring up children is to love them for what they are, and not for what anyone thinks they ought to be. In this world no two human beings are exactly alike, even identical twins behave differently, in spite of apparently the same genetic endowment. Every child, in some respects, is like all other children, but in some ways like no other. Understanding and respecting the uniqueness of each child is the key to success.

Some children are highly organised, meticulous, and confident, while others are extremely disorganised, negligent, and timid. The first group is able to cope with the stresses of examinations, stage presentations, and other events with consummate ease. The other group is unable to face even minor strains; during an examination they may become so nervous that they make a mess of even those answers they have committed to memory. They need careful handling and emotional backing, with a comprehensive support system developed and deployed to not only overcome their weaknesses but to help them develop a positive attitude.

If parents are conscious about the concept of uniqueness, problems emerging from unwarranted and unjustified comparisons between children (with the potential to damage a child's personality, seriously and permanently) can be avoided.

Parents cite the example of children good in studies or sports, in the fond hope that their own children will be motivated to perform better. If this is done judiciously and skilfully, it might help, but insensitivity can undermine a child's confidence and self-esteem. Without even realising it, parents can make children feel inferior and unwanted by praising their siblings or peers. This is especially damaging if done in the background of constant criticism of the child. As a consequence, instead of improving, the child's performance will deteriorate further.

Why do some children fail, in spite of the potential and favourable conditions, while others succeed despite all adversities? It is apparent, in the case of the latter group, that the strengths, and a remarkable resilience in their physical, temperamental, and psychological make-up, drive them to victory. They triumph over obstacles in ways that can surprise us.

Charlie Chaplin was abandoned by his mother and placed in an orphanage when he was a little child. He overcame his emotional trauma to become a successful actor. He seems to have turned his own early life predicament to advantage by playing 'the tramp'.

It is now well established that *a sense of uniqueness builds self-esteem*. Parents must understand that uniqueness and high self-esteem are interconnected, as well as interdependent. If they can make a child feel unique and special, they have scored a huge victory.

To develop a sense of uniqueness, children need to know that there is something special about them, that they can do specific things that no one else can do, and they need others to acknowledge this uniqueness too. If children are given opportunities to use their imagination and creativity, and allowed to express themselves in their own unique way, their personalities will blossom. Children who feel good about their personal characteristics, gain confidence and approach situations and challenges more positively. They start making efforts to improve their lot, and succeed in receiving approval and respect for their accomplishments.

When a child starts appreciating her own capabilities and learns to enjoy being different, she becomes destined for glory.

7 STEPS TO BUILD YOUR CHILD'S SENSE OF UNIQUENESS

1. Accept your child

Accepting the child in toto—the good and the bad—is the first step towards acknowledging her uniqueness. While you may focus on changing undesirable behaviour, you should not insist upon changing everything about the child—lest you rob her of her uniqueness trying to mould her into your own ideals. It is important that you communicate your acceptance to your child by appreciating her assets and praising her accomplishments. You must provide her with opportunities to explain her feelings, attitudes, opinions, and actions. This can clear many doubts and misunderstandings between you. Remember, acceptance of uniqueness is the key to self-esteem.

2. Point out the potential

Parents should train themselves to recognise their children's unique abilities and talents, and point them out to them. If you find your daughter sings well, tell her about her gift and try to nurture her talent. Similarly, children may be gifted at chess, computers, mathematics, tennis, cricket, and so on. They can develop their unique talents into extremely profitable careers provided they receive proper guidance and necessary assistance from their parents.

3. Let children do things their own way

Most parents, if they see their child writing with the left hand, force her into using the right hand due to wrong beliefs and taboos. By inducing a natural left-hander into becoming a right-hander, they only end up confusing the child and her brain.

Each child has a different way of doing things. Ankita, aged eleven, preferred to take medicines in the form of tablets. Even when she was a three-year-old kid she could easily swallow pills of various sizes. Her older sister, Aparajita, aged thirteen, till date chokes at the very sight of a tablet. She must have her medicines as syrups, which need to be given in large quantities because she weighs over 40 kgs.

The message is clear: *don't tamper with the child's basic temperament*. Personality traits need modification only if they are likely to harm the child's future prospects.

4. Allow children to express themselves creatively

For diverse reasons, some children have a low sense of being uniquely gifted. They normally aver that they are not good at, or can't achieve, anything. Parents should not take these statements lightly, as they denote that the child is facing serious problems with her self-esteem. Before these feelings blow up into a full-grown inferiority complex, parents should try to identify areas in which she has a special interest. If she can paint, arrange flowers, sing, or play an instrument—she should be motivated to take it up as a hobby. At the same time, they should bolster her sense of uniqueness by praising her work.

5. Treat each child as an individual

There are umpteen examples of parents with two kids who are exact opposites in all respects. They have obviously inherited the same set of genes, which interact with the same environmental set-up, then why this difference? It has been postulated that even subtle differences in gene patterns can cause major behavioural differences.

Keeping this fact in mind, parents should prepare themselves to find apples and oranges growing on the same tree. If parents treat apples as apples, and enjoy oranges for being oranges, they will harvest a successful crop.

6. Facilitate your child's learning style

Some children put on music when they are studying; others want pindrop silence. Some wake up early in the morning, while others study late into the night. Parents must identify and support the child's style of learning, provided it is producing the desired results. Trying to alter the preferred way of learning may adversely affect the child's academic performance.

We have seen parents asking/forcing the child to read quietly, while she prefers to read aloud because she can remember facts better this way. Parents should understand that some children need both visual and auditory inputs to memorise information.

7. Loving each child best

'Since he was about three, everything to do with Jatin has been a struggle,' recalls Mrs Bhandari. 'The first word he ever spoke was "No", and he is still stuck with it. Before a gift is even given, he is negotiating the next one. When study time arrives he throws a tantrum, when it's dinnertime he suddenly loses his appetite, and when it's party time he fails to find a single good dress. He seems to take pride in his capacity to send me into a fit.'

She further adds, 'Jatin never lets any chance go a-begging. If his younger brother, Nitin, got a bigger piece of chocolate, he would go to the extent of measuring it with a scale. His teachers are always nicer to his classmates than to him. He is on a constant vigil for any injustice to him, no matter how slight or unintentional. Nitin, on the other hand, is as easy to care for as Jatin is difficult. He is organised, self-sufficient, responsible, and helpful. Unlike Jatin he doesn't need constant reminders for bathing, having breakfast, completing home work, and other tasks.'

Mrs Bhandari says, 'I sometimes think, do I love Nitin more? I blame myself for not being a better mother, and more appreciative of and responsive to the needs of Jatin. How many times have I promised myself, I will never yell at Jatin like a mad person again; I'll try to remain calm. Moments later I am hollering at him using both my lungs to the fullest.'

Many parents face a similar predicament, but there is no need to feel guilty or miserable. You love your children with passion, each for very different reasons. If you have one easygoing child, feel happy for this little mercy God has bestowed upon you. The other more difficult one has been sent to you lest you develop a misguided belief: 'Parenting isn't so hard after all.'

11

Group Activities Develop Bonding and Leadership

A single-child family is becoming quite the norm these days, depriving the child of the values of shared experiences with siblings. Long durations of studies, career development, late marriages, and delayed childbirth have led to this status; parents find one or two children a handful, so handling more seems too daunting. In the past, if there were fewer children in a family, there were numerous cousins to interact with. Today, with leave constraints and long-distance travel, even in close-knit families interaction with cousins is limited, though it may exist on electronic social networking platforms.

In such a scenario, group activities become necessary, and good schools take the initiative to organise such opportunities. But, usually, parents try to keep their child away from these, not realising that it goes against the overall scheme of bringing up a smart child.

Group activities help in developing the following qualities:

- ✔ Increased friendliness, and sharing of personal problems
- ✔ Acceptance of membership in the team
- ✔ Ability to express criticism constructively
- ✔ Accepting and using fruitfully honest and caring feedback
- ✔ Attempting to achieve harmony by avoiding conflict
- ✔ A sense of cohesion, team spirit, and shared goals with other human beings
- ✔ Establishing and maintaining ground rules and boundaries in a social group

SOME GROUP ACTIVITIES FOR YOUR CHILD

Excursions

The best activity for children is by way of excursions—to city museums and parks, or tours to different cities or countries. Schools usually plan such outings as an extension of their educational programme. They are designed to allow children to explore their physical and social environment. Well-planned excursions require planning and preparation to ensure adequate care and safety of the children, and should incorporate the management of any possible risks in familiar or unfamiliar environments. Hence it is critical for schools to hold one or two meetings with the parents prior to the excursion. If the school doesn't do this, then you must be proactive and interact with the school administration on these counts, yourself.

Excursions should provide children with age-appropriate fun, and recreational and challenging experiences, together with a fair amount of freedom within predetermined limits. There should be opportunities for them to learn valuable life skills too. All this is not exactly simple, but if designed well, it is easier to achieve.

Methodical planning means...

The excursion should be planned thoroughly, and the managing team of teachers and attendants should carry the following items at the minimum:

- A suitably equipped first aid kit
- Telephone numbers of persons to be notified of any accident, injury, trauma, or illness
- Operational mobile phone with an appropriate connection to a network and/or internet
- Appropriate instructions and medications for children with chronic illnesses like asthma, epilepsy, diabetes, or allergies
- Other essential and need-based items such as sunscreen lotions, hats, food, and water

Parents should also know...

- The proposed route and destination of the excursion
- The means of transport
- The number of adults and children, given the risks posed
- The number of responsible adults for supervision, and whether any specialised skills are required to ensure children's safety
- The proposed activities
- The likely duration of the excursion
- Any hazards and risks associated with water-based activities

Summer camps

This is a new trend that has become fairly popular with working parents. Several organisations, including many schools, hold summer camps during school vacations, generally for four to six weeks, thereby covering a major chunk of the summer break.

These camps have two advantages:

1. Children are kept busy during the daytime while, simultaneously, getting exposed to a host of new activities, which they would not be able to experience during the busy academic session.
2. Parents don't have to worry about their children while they are at work.

These camps are so designed that children learn several skills under one roof. Some of the popular activities on offer are:

- Drawing/Painting/Arts and Craft
- Music—Vocal/Instrumental
- Dance—Indian/Western
- Computer and Internet Operations
- Public speaking
- Aerobics/Yoga
- Swimming
- Skating
- Basketball
- Shooting
- Horse-riding

Arpita loved splashing around in the small water tank in her house. Fortunately, she had a chance to attend a summer camp organised by a leading school in her town. Not only did she sharpen her computer skills, but she also received swimming lessons from a qualified coach. She turned out to be a quick learner, and by the end of the camp, was unbeatable in the 50-metres freestyle and breaststroke events. Her father got her a membership in the swimming pool near their home, where she continued to practise diligently, and soon her source of pleasure turned into a serious commitment. She became the state swimming champion in her age group in the 50-metres freestyle, and went on to participate at the national level.

Arpita's story could be your daughter's too. It is these small initiatives and opportunities, provided by parents, which make an enormous difference in a child's life.

Team games

Cricket, football, hockey, and basketball are some of the popular team games. A team consists of a group of players with different talents but with a similar goal—to win, by outperforming their opponents. Towards this end, they guide, facilitate, and support each other. In football, if the goalkeeper is beaten, other defenders will jump in to stop the ball from entering the goalpost. In cricket, if the top order batsmen fail, the lower order consisting mainly of bowlers will try to get as many runs as they can. These are just two examples of how players provide a cover to their teammates.

Team games instil the habit of out-of-the-box thinking, build camaraderie, and develop a never-say-die spirit. These are the qualities that matter greatly in real life situations too, differentiating the also-rans from the winners.

Anshul and Amish were the stars of their school cricket team. They made an extremely successful opening partnership, and were largely instrumental in their school winning the district interschool cricket tournament. Their partnership broke up as they went their separate ways to different colleges, but their friendship continued. After college, they restarted their partnership, this time not on the field, but in business. They obtained bank finance and opened a transformer-manufacturing unit, which is doing quite well, as is their partnership.

NCC—National Cadet Corps

A commendable school activity is the NCC. It aims at developing character, comradeship, discipline, a secular outlook, a spirit of adventure, and ideals of selfless service. It creates organised, trained, and motivated youngsters with leadership qualities in all walks of life.

Other options

Besides excursions, summer camps, and other outdoor activities, several indoor pastimes are available within the school premises, or in the city. In case one's neighbourhood lacks the facilities for group activities, the parents should get together and organise them within their own group. Resident Welfare Associations (RWAs) can plan social functions for children of the vicinity to come together and share the stage.

12

The Go, Grow, Glow Nutrients

Childhood nutrition, one of the most contentious issues in practically all households, has always been a subject of much discussion and research. The mother and her mother-in-law are always at loggerheads about what is good for the child and what isn't. Till a decade or two ago, the mother-in-law usually prevailed by citing her experiences of childcare. But that advantage is now redundant, thanks to the several good books on child-rearing in the market, and of course, the information freely available on the internet.

Equipped with this knowledge, the mother feels that she is better qualified in matters related to child nutrition. While this may be true to some extent, a total dismissal of age-old traditions and child-rearing practices is fraught with danger. Over-dependence on the internet may not only compromise the child's health, but also, the mother may worry if the child's intake does not match the recommendations.

Whew! Did that confuse you? Well that wasn't the intention. All we want is that you strike a balance between traditional wisdom and contemporary child feeding practices, as you are likely to get the best results if you combine the two.

Children are small but their nutritional needs are big. They require more nutrition in relation to their size to fulfil their demands for growth, body maintenance, and physical activity. If adequate calories are not available, their growth falters and they become lethargic. According to UNDP studies, 45–55 per cent of children have an inadequate diet. In India, 70 per cent of children consume less calories per day than the RDA (Recommended Dietary Allowance), the percentage varying in different age groups. Almost 43 per cent of children in India are underweight, an indication of less calorie consumption.

The nutritional requirement of each child varies, and is governed by genetic and metabolic differences. The usual parental lament about their child's intake being meagre as compared to other children must be explained in the light of the above fact. The basic goals in childhood nutrition are the achievement of satisfactory growth parameters, and avoidance of nutritional deficiency conditions.

Good nutrition helps to prevent acute and chronic illnesses, develop physical and mental potentialities, and provide reserves for times of stress. For convenience's sake, we can divide various foodstuffs into three broad categories: Go, Grow, and Glow Nutrients.

GO NUTRIENTS

Carbohydrates and fats come into this category. They provide energy for physical activity and growth, but there is no evidence that either carbohydrate or fat is a superior source of energy. Energy requirement is expressed per unit of body weight. An infant requires approximately three times more energy than an adult.

A. Carbohydrates

Carbohydrates contain four calories per gram. About 50 to 60 per cent of total daily calories should come from carbohydrates, which the human body converts into glucose—the quickest source of energy that can be used instantly.

Carbohydrates are also stored in the liver in the form of glycogen, to be utilised whenever needed. However, there is a limit to the amount that can be stored, and once that limit is reached, the body turns the extra carbohydrates into fat. This fat initially accumulates around the tummy and buttocks, but if carbohydrate excess continues, the fat starts getting deposited around the shoulders, neck, and face. So one does not need to eat only fatty food to get fat; even excessive intake of carbohydrates can result in overweight.

There are two types of carbohydrates: *healthy* and *relatively unhealthy*.

Healthy carbohydrates. Multigrain bread, oats, unpolished rice, lentils, beans, among other food items constitute this class. Also known as complex or slower-acting carbohydrates, they have a complex chemical structure and take longer to get metabolised. Thus the level of blood sugar rises slowly and remains near normal for longer periods. (These carbs are especially helpful for obese children because they avert hunger for longer periods too.)

Relatively unhealthy carbohydrates. Candy, cookies, cake, ice cream soda, juice, sweetened beverages, and so on fall into this group. They are also known as simple or fast-acting carbohydrates, with a simple chemical structure, and which are metabolised rapidly. Thus the blood sugar level rises rapidly, but doesn't last very long. That is why these carbohydrates work well to correct low blood sugar conditions, but don't satisfy hunger as satisfactorily as healthy carbohydrates do. The implications are pretty obvious: if the hunger is not satisfied, the child will keep eating more of these foods and will end up with the problem of obesity.

B. Fats

Fats, of all nutrients, carry the most calories: nine per gram. In a healthy diet, not more than 30 per cent of total daily calories should come from fat. This means restricting fats to 40 to 70 grams per day, depending on the age and weight of the individual.

Fats are broken down into fatty acids by the metabolic process. Currently, two fatty acids—arachidonic acid and docosahexaenoic acid (DHA)—are in focus. These two fatty acids are most prevalent in the central nervous system and the latter comprises up to 40 per cent of the fatty acid content of retinal photoreceptor membranes. The generally better visual and cognitive development of breast-fed (vs formula-fed) children has been attributed to the presence of these fatty acids in human milk. To overcome this handicap, some formula milk powders now come fortified with DHA.

There are various types of fats, some healthier than others. Go for mono-unsaturated, or poly-unsaturated, fats. These fats are liquid at room temperature, for example, olive, canola, and nut oils. Mono-unsaturated fats are especially healthy because they lower the bad cholesterol (LDL—Low Density Lipids) in the blood.

Right from the beginning, saturated and trans-fats must be restricted in a child's diet. Saturated fats are found in foods that come from animals, such as meat and dairy products. Solid at room temperature, these fats can damage the heart and arteries in the long run. They also include coconut or palm kernel oils, and hydrogenated oils as well.

Trans-fats are found in most processed foods and many fried fast-foods, such as french fries. They help food stay fresh longer, but are just as harmful as saturated fat; the reason why paediatricians ask parents to keep their children away from junk food. In India we are fighting two nutritional wars!...one against 'MALNUTRITION' and the other against 'MALL-NUTRITION'.

GROW NUTRIENTS

Like carbohydrates, the protein requirement of infants and children is also greater per unit of body weight than for adults. The human body needs proteins for growth, maintenance, and energy. Proteins are the building blocks which form all tissues and organs of the body. They contain four calories per gram. Although not the primary source of energy, in a healthy diet 10 to 15 per cent of total daily calories should come from proteins. They can also be stored by our bodies and are used mostly by our muscles.

Proteins can be broadly divided into two types—from animal sources and from plant sources. Animal proteins are nutritionally superior to plant proteins, because they are easier to metabolise and assimilate. Before assimilation, proteins are broken down into amino acids within the body. There are nine essential amino acids, which must be provided in the diet because the body cannot synthesise them. The rest, because the body can manufacture them, are called non-essential amino acids.

Plant proteins. Pulses and legumes are a rich source of proteins. But because their amino acid pattern is not ideal for the human body, their bioavailability is poor. Soybeans are a particularly good source. Modern preparations of soy protein are of very high quality and are used in many infant formulas, especially for children who have chronic diarrhoea due to lactose intolerance. Soy protein has insufficient methionine, but when it is fortified with this, it becomes a first rate protein.

Animal proteins. Milk, cheese, eggs, fish, chicken, and meat are all excellent sources. Of course, breast milk, *is* the best nutrition for babies. In fact, the quality of any protein is defined in accordance with how closely its amino acid pattern resembles that of human milk. Human milk contains only one gram protein per 100 ml. So, to meet the current RDA of 2.0 grams/kg/day, about 200 ml/kg/day must be ingested. But even if the baby is consuming less, she will not develop a protein deficiency because of the high quality and easy digestibility of human milk.

Eggs are an easily available source of quality protein. The amino acid pattern of egg protein (albumin) is ideally suited for humans. Incidences of Kwashiorkor (a protein deficiency state) have decreased considerably due to the increased consumption of eggs and milk.

Role of health drinks. Several companies aggressively advertise their protein health drinks. Tall claims, literally, are made about their effectiveness in promoting the growth and development of children. While they may provide some protein, their ability to make the child taller or brainier is highly disputable. Instead of investing in such exorbitantly priced commercial protein brands, it is advisable that you provide the child wholesome home-cooked meals rich in proteins.

GLOW NUTRIENTS

Minerals and Vitamins make up this segment. They are essential for various metabolic processes, for maintaining the immune system, and vital for a healthy, glowing look. Although required in minute amounts, they play an important role in the overall functioning of the body.

Minerals

There is a long list—iron, zinc, copper, manganese, chromium, molybdenum, selenium, and others that are needed by the human body. Most of them are present in a normal diet, and their deficiency is relatively uncommon, except for iron. Iron is an important mineral whose deficiency results in anaemia. The new-born infant has a sufficient iron store for the first four months. The red blood cells (RBC) also have a life span of four months (120 days). After this period the iron need of the baby starts increasing on two counts—1. The iron stores begin to get depleted. 2. The life span of the RBCs present at the time of birth is over and new RBCs are to be formed, which requires iron. The baby's diet has insufficient quantities of iron so if iron supplementation is not started around four months, chances of the baby becoming anaemic are high.

Vitamins

Vitamins are essential nutrients that must be supplied either through a well-balanced diet or via the large number of multivitamin syrups available in the market. When used judiciously, they can help the child grow. Let's take a look at some of the important vitamins:

Vitamin A is present in whole milk, milk fat products, egg yolk, green leafy vegetables, and yellow fruits and vegetables. Fish liver oils are a very rich source of this vitamin. Its deficiency leads to night blindness, corneal damage, defective tooth enamel, retarded growth, and impaired resistance to infection.

Vitamin B Complex is a group of vitamins:

Vitamin B_1, or Thiamine, is present in whole grain, wheat germ, legumes, and nuts. Liver and meat are also good sources. The deficiency of this vitamin causes a disease known as beriberi; therefore, it is also called the anti-beriberi vitamin. Fatigue, irritability, loss of appetite, constipation, insomnia, headache, and a rapid heart rate are some of the other symptoms observed with thiamine deficiency.

Vitamin B_2, or Riboflavin, is present in milk, cheese, eggs, liver, meat, fish, green leafy vegetables, and whole grains.

Its deficiency causes photophobia, blurred vision, itching, and burning of the eyes, and poor growth.

Vitamin B_6, or Pyridoxine, is present in meat, liver, whole grains, soybeans, nuts, fish, eggs, and green vegetables. Its deficiency causes irritability, convulsions, and anaemia.

Vitamin B_{12}, or Cyanocobalamin, is obtained from meat, fish, eggs, milk, and cheese. Its deficiency causes a type of anaemia, which only responds to the vitamin being injected into the body. It is also used to treat disorders of the nerves.

Niacin is present in meat, fish, poultry, liver, whole grains, peanuts, and green vegetables. Its deficiency causes Pellagra characterised by three Ds—diarrhoea, dementia, and dermatitis.

Folic acid is obtained mainly from plant sources—green vegetables, nuts, cereals, fruit, yeast, beans, and peas. Anaemia, mouth ulcers, and redness of the tongue are a consequence of folic acid deficiency.

Biotin is present in yeast and animal products. Its deficiency causes dermatitis and dandruff.

Vitamin C is present in citrus fruits, tomatoes, berries, cabbage, and green vegetables. Cooking has a destructive effect on this vitamin, which underscores the importance of eating salads. Vitamin C deficiency causes scurvy, the most prominent feature of which is bleeding gums. Its lack also leads to poor healing of wounds.

Vitamin D is also called the sunshine vitamin. When our body is exposed to sunlight, the Vitamin D precursor present in the skin is converted to Vitamin D. Going by this logic, in a country like India, with plenty of sunshine, there should be no cases of Vitamin D deficiency. Unfortunately, this is not so.

Over the past few years, the incidence of Vitamin D deficiency has increased manifold in our country, due to a sedentary and indoor lifestyle. Instead of parks, children go to malls; instead of outdoor games, they play computer games in bedrooms. From home to car to school and back to home—a child (for that matter even an adult: replace school with office) barely steps out into the sun.

Vitamin D helps in the regulation of almost one thousand genes in our body. It plays an important role in calcium metabolism, the neuromuscular system, and body resistance to various infections. Its deficiency leads to poor bone and teeth formation, growth retardation, and in severe cases, rickets. A large number of foods enriched with this vitamin are available in the market. Infants should be given 200 IU/day, while older children can be administered a daily dose of 400 to 800 IU. Treatment should continue for prolonged periods and, simultaneously, necessary lifestyle changes must also be introduced.

Vitamin E is present in germ oils of various seeds, green leafy vegetables, nuts, and legumes. It is an antioxidant and helps maintain the integrity of various membranes.

Vitamin K is widely distributed across various foods, green leafy vegetables being a good source. It plays an important role in the process of blood coagulation, and its deficiency can lead to haemorrhagic manifestations.

We are sure that you are now brimming with knowledge regarding the essential nutrients and are itching to feed them to your child. There is an old saying that: you can bring the horse to the water, but you can't make him drink. The same applies here. You can prepare a good, well-balanced meal for your child, but the real challenge is to make her eat it. We are giving you some strategic advice to help you to not only bring the child to the table, but to also make her eat.

TIPS TO GET YOUR CHILD TO GO, GROW, GLOW

So many parents are worried about their child's total lack of interest in eating anything nutritionists would consider 'healthy food'. And of course, the issue has become more complicated due to the easy availability of fast/junk food these days. Here are some tips to make your child get maximum nutrition with the minimum struggle:

Milk is important

Milk is important for the growth of a child. In fact, it is

called a *complete food* because it contains almost all the essential nutrients required to grow optimally. Most of us parents battle our children, every day, to make them drink sufficient quantities of milk. But, did you know that the exact same nutritional benefits can be provided to them even through preparations they adore?...(Milk hidden in) kheer, hot cereals, custard, and other milk desserts...Did you know that a cup of low-fat yogurt, or a slice of cheese—which they will surely eat—has the same amount of calcium as in a glass of milk?

Scientific research has shown that *lactase*, the enzyme essential for the proper digestion of milk, may be present in sub-optimal quantities in certain children, who develop abdominal colic, bloating, or belching on the consumption of milk. If your child frequently complains of nausea, or vomits, after drinking milk, she may be *lactase*-deficient. In this case, reduce the quantity of milk to no more than one cup at a time, or try giving it in the form of curds, cheese, and other milk-based preparations.

Vegetables are needed

Rare is the child who never shows an aversion to vegetables. 'My daughter picked them off her plate and lined them up on the dining table to make a point,' declared Amita Sharma as she entered the consultation chamber. This was the net result of our advice to add vegetables to noodles, her daughter Mini's staple diet.

Probably ladies' fingers and potatoes are among the few vegetables uniformly liked by all children. You immediately join the league of a lucky parent if your child likes fruit, as they provide many of the same vitamins and minerals as vegetables do. Juices count too, but you should vary the choices and serve fresh fruit juice instead of preservative-containing commercial preparations. Since too much juice can decrease appetite and cause diarrhoea, serve no more than 250 ml a day.

You have hit the jackpot if your child likes soup! The possibilities are enormous and you can put practically any vegetable into it. Grate them fine, or even better—mash them up to an unrecognisable state. Ignorance is bliss! Even children who abhor vegetables may consume the soup version.

Many children add sauce to whatever they eat: you can add puréed vegetables to that bottle of tomato sauce kept permanently on your dining table!

Fast food is a problem

Pizza, french fries, burgers, noodles, rolls, and a variety of fried foods, have become the staple diet of most children. They will eat only if the food is deep-fried. The problem is that fast foods are constituted mostly of starch, fat, and salt. Like adults, kids over three years should get no more than 30 per cent of their daily calories from fat.

One way to balance their total fat intake is to use

skimmed milk and low-fat cheese in general. Give them a bowl of cut fruit such as orange sections and apple slices, before dinnertime. Munching on these makes kids less likely to gorge on greasy foods later. Healthy versions of fast-foods can be made at home, for example, oven-fried chicken, pizza with low-fat mozzarella cheese, microwaved popcorn, and so on.

Sweets should be restricted

Nimmi loves chocolates, candies, ice cream, shakes, biscuits, and other confectionery—for that matter, even plain sugar. Her mother tried to ban sweets, which resulted in Nimmi devouring them on the sly.

A ban is not going to work if your fridge and larder are loaded with sweets; it would only make them more desirable. Forbidding is not the solution; instead, allowing an occasional chocolate or ice cream will reduce the craving and result in decreased consumption of sweets. Parents and other family members must set an example by going slow on sweets themselves.

Snacking must be controlled

Many children prefer intermittent snacking to regimented meals. If not controlled, the snackers will eventually become meal-skippers. Although snacks are necessary, since most kids cannot go from lunch to dinner without them, skipping meals will deny them a balanced diet.

Gross snacking will result in a deficiency of vitamins and minerals, and overloading of calories, resulting in obesity (weight management is all about balancing calories-in and calories-out).

You shouldn't make children give up on snacking altogether; instead provide them with low-fat, low-calorie items, say of a hundred calories or less per serving. A child could choose up to one snack before lunch, two between lunch and dinner, and one after dinner.

The best way to make kids eat right is to have interesting but healthy foods available at home. For this, a basic knowledge of the nutritional profile of common food items is essential. Also, if you eat right, your children will probably end up eating right too.

ROLE OF APPETITE STIMULANTS

Loss of appetite occurs as the first symptom of almost all diseases. Throat infection (tonsillitis, pharyngitis), oral ulcers, ear infection, viral infections, measles, mumps, gastritis, urinary infection, and others lead to acute anorexia in children.

Opinion regarding the use of drugs to stimulate appetite in children, is divided; some doctors use them, others don't. The main argument against their use is that the effect is temporary; as soon as the drug is stopped the appetite is lost again. Moreover, no drug is without its side effects.

The most commonly prescribed appetite stimulant is

cyproheptadine. Introduced in the market as an anti-allergic drug, it was later found to induce voracious appetites in its users. (It also causes intense sedation.)

Buclizine hydrochloride, available as Longifene, is another commonly used appetite stimulant, and syrups containing Tricholine citrate and Sorbitol solution are known to stimulate appetites too.

Tonics with multivitamins, minerals, and iron may also help, and several Ayurvedic preparations are claimed to be effective as well.

13
Teaching at Home

An exasperated Mrs Saini, and her fatigued twelve-year-old daughter Deepika, are sitting at the dining table struggling to finish the never-ending course of study for the forthcoming terminal exams. The hot, humid August evening makes them sweat profusely, adding to their woes. They have been at it all evening; they haven't had dinner, and have finished with only three of the ten chapters from the prescribed social studies textbook. More than Deepika, it's her mother who is panicking at the prospect of her daughter faring badly in the exam.

It's a cold December night; the time 10.00 p.m. A tired Mr Sahni and his bored son Kunal are staring blankly at the pile of homework in front of them. The maths assignment is still incomplete and, on top of that, there is craftwork to be done as well...

Every night, in millions of homes across the country, similar scenes are enacted with alarming regularity. The actors may be different but the script usually remains the same. The present curriculum in most schools necessitates teaching at home, and with both parents working, this takes a heavy toll on their mental and physical resources.

Although the problem of homework is not a new phenomenon, the pressure of the modern educational system has turned it into a recurring nightmare for most families. Homework has degenerated into a form of forced labour, in which pages upon pages of work are heaped upon the child, with hardly any scope for improvisation or originality. The sad part is that the child is expected to work like a slave, but an even greater tragedy is that it also enslaves the parents, who have to sit beside the child helping her along.

And the irony is that most teachers know how well nigh impossible it is for a child to cope with such copious amounts of work, and yet they saddle her with more and more. Many, with young kids of their own, are also aware of who is actually doing much of the homework. This malpractice has prevailed over the last fifty years, yet nothing is being done to curtail it.

The main sources of stress for young children are:

- Waking up very early for school
- Long bus journey to and from school
- Multiple tuitions
- Voluminous homework
- Unit tests, term and final exams

- Projects (usually compiled through paid sources)
- Social pressures—birthday parties, socialising by parents.

There are innumerable children who encounter such sustained stress day in and day out. Imagine the plight of a child who doesn't perform well even after such a backbreaking schedule. Think about the parents who work throughout the day and on coming back home, sit for hours with their children helping them with their homework. It is not difficult to visualise the frustrations of highly qualified parents who teach molecular biology and genetics during the day and regress to teaching 'A cow has four legs' in the evening! Most parents are always prepared to assist and work alongside their children on homework. In spite of their busy schedule they are ready to take out time to teach their wards, especially during exams. Credit must be given for this! As far as helping the child academically is concerned, the dedication of new-age parents is at par or maybe even greater than the previous generation of parents.

While teaching, the approach and methodology of parents may vary—some restricting themselves to brief occasional explanations, with others going to the extent of completing the entire task themselves. It's the children who are primarily responsible for this difference in parental approach; some are by nature sincere, hardworking, and able to cope without much supervision or help; others have studies at the bottom of their agenda, if at all. This latter group is immune to parental cajoling or reasoning, and often, even threats and bribery fail to convince them to study. While struggling to bring these children to book, parents should take care not to become frustrated or disappointed.

TEACHING AT HOME SUCCESSFULLY

Teaching at home has two components:

A. Making the child do homework on a regular basis
B. Helping the child prepare for exams

Doing homework daily inculcates the habit of regular studies. This disciplined approach is very helpful in the long run when the course load increases (and in fact, once the child grows up and starts working too).

Studying for the exams is an all-together different ball game. It requires a more focused and concerted effort, with meticulous planning in which parents have an important role to play.

A. Tips to tackle homework

1. Fix the time for homework. In most schools, loads of homework is given to children on a daily basis. If there is no fixed schedule for doing it, it will either remain incomplete or be done haphazardly at the last moment, creating anxiety for both—the child and the parent. It is best to give the child the liberty to decide the time for homework. Some children prefer to do it as soon as they return from school; others may choose a time later in the evening. However, once the slot is fixed, it should be adhered to as realistically as possible. Parents must ensure that during this period, no interruptions in the form of phone calls, TV, or visitors are allowed.

Initially, parents may have to remind the child of the time for homework, but gradually this will become a habit. Once this happens, the daily pleadings, chidings, and threats may not be required and this should improve the parent–child relationship as well.

2. Don't begin with the toughest assignment. If children have four assignments to do, let them finish the three easier ones first. This makes them feel happy and relaxed because they now have only one assignment left; and with their confidence boosted, they can tackle this tougher one with greater assurance to boot. On the contrary, if the child starts with a difficult task, she may either get bogged down with it, or spend the entire time in finishing that single assignment alone. This may give rise to frustration and feelings of inadequacy.

3. An alternate strategy. Most teachers and parents recommend reading through a chapter before trying to solve the questions from it. We think it's a good idea to read the questions before reading the chapter. By using this strategy, the child will have an idea of what she should be looking for in the chapter, and what to concentrate on while reading through it. Suggest to her that she mark with a pencil the passages that seem related to the given questions. This way, she will be able to pinpoint relevant and important information in the first reading itself, and this will help her when she refers back to several pages in search of answers.

4. Reduce dependency. Parents should try to avoid sitting next to the child while she is doing her homework. This is easier said than done because most children stop working the moment the parent's attention is diverted. It's not that they can't work—rather, they choose not to. Once the child develops this dependency, she is unable to function independently in the classroom as well, and brings home unfinished classwork, on top of the homework. After a busy, tiring day, when parents are faced with the prospect of sitting long hours over their child's homework, they are, understandably, likely to lose their temper.

If you are trapped in this situation where your child refuses to work on her own, you should get her used to working independently in stages. Initially, sit at the far end of the room for a few days. Then start moving out of the room for brief spells, and gradually increase the period of your absences until the child is working alone.

There is no fixed age when children should be given the responsibility of their own study. It is generally through a trial-and-error method that parents come to know when the child is ready to take independent charge. This, however, does not mean that they shouldn't keep track of the child's study schedule. In fact, the child will always need suggestions, supervision, and support, at every stage of her academic career.

5. Don't zero in on mistakes first. While checking the child's homework, first praise her for the correct answers, or for the right spellings of difficult words. For the incorrect ones, don't use criticism. Instead say, 'Please check these again, I am sure you will get the correct answers.' The child will not feel offended and will redo the problems with confidence.

Some parents have a habit of zeroing in on the incorrect work first. This makes them angry, and the resulting outburst upsets the child too. She may develop feelings of animosity or helplessness, and her work—instead of improving—may actually deteriorate.

6. Split the assignment. Most children benefit if the assignment is divided into smaller parts, and immediate feedback given on each part completed. Let your child solve three problems and then come back to you for checking them. Give encouragement for the correct answers and send her back to do the next lot. By providing immediate feedback and approval, you motivate her to tackle the next task with renewed vigour. Another advantage is that in case she has begun on the wrong track, the error can be detected and explained right at the start, saving her from having to repeat the entire assignment again.

Once the child's homework is checked and done, she will have a feeling of accomplishment and a sense of security knowing the work is correct. This makes her more confident in the class, and her academic performance may improve substantially.

7. Use multiple modes of input. Children retain information better if it is provided through multiple sensory inputs. It has been observed that a combination of auditory and visual inputs is more effective than any one of them alone. Parents can tape-record some especially bothersome chapters so that the child can listen and read simultaneously. They can record a favourite song or joke in between to cheer up the child.

8. Don't overreact. Grimaces, sighs, raising of eyebrows, throwing up of hands—some parents behave as if they are enacting a tragic scene rather than helping the child with homework. Don't hit your forehead with your hand, and please don't hyperventilate while teaching your child. Negative body language must be avoided because it only adds to the tension. If parents allow themselves to become agitated they will make the child anxious, and undermine her ability to perform satisfactorily.

9. Avoid doing your child's homework. Some parents don't have the time or patience to sit for hours waiting for the child to complete the homework. Others may feel the assignment is too difficult for her to handle. Whatever the reason, when parents finish their child's homework, the end result is always damaging, because the child develops a feeling of inadequacy and failure, and may become increasingly dependent on the parents for her academic work.

10. It's better to end the agony. If the child has been working on her assignment for quite some time without making any worthwhile progress, it's better to end her agony by putting a stop to the homework. What the child has not accomplished in thirty minutes, she is unlikely to achieve in the next three hours and thirty minutes either. Making the child sit indefinitely at work will only strengthen her feelings of incompetence. If this happens once in a while you shouldn't get worried: but if it is a pattern, you should start looking for the cause of her inability, and take remedial measures.

Inability to cope with homework

S.No.	Probable Cause	Remedy
1.	The child may not have understood the concept in class and therefore, is not	Write a note to the teacher explaining the circumstances. Your

able to finish the assignment at home.	meeting with the teacher may help the child.
2. The child may already have developed feelings of helplessness and dependency and may wait for you to complete the assignment.	Try to facilitate independent working. Work towards building the child's confidence and improving her academic self-concept.
3. The child may be suffering from a learning disability.	Take the help of a child counsellor. Consult a person trained in developmental paediatrics.

B. Helping the child to prepare for exams

1. Emphasise the need for extra effort. Parents should motivate the child to put in an additional two to four hours of daily study during the exam period. Extra hours will naturally vary according to the grade in which the child is studying; the higher the grade the more the time needed. For board exams, good students spend their every free minute studying. While it is advisable to stimulate the child to study hard, caution must be taken not to exercise unnecessary pressure. Coercion usually proves counterproductive, and may lead to a drop in academic performance.

2. Cut down on socialising. During the exams, parents should try to cut down on their social commitments.

While there will always be important engagements and events which must be attended, it is the frivolous socialising which they must avoid. In this way, parents show their involvement and solidarity with their child during this stressful period. This will not only make her more serious about her studies, it will also make her more committed.

3. The early burn-out phenomenon. It is somewhat similar to the expression 'peaking early' used commonly in sports. A team that performs superbly in the earlier rounds fizzles out later, resulting in its exit during the quarter or semifinal of the tournament. Help your child prepare for the exams in such a manner that her study hours and performance increase gradually and peak during the exams. If she reaches saturation point by the time the exams start, she is unlikely to perform to her best potential.

4. Reverse approach. Once the exam timetable is given to the child, sit down with her and work out the number of days needed to prepare for each subject. This will depend upon the child's relative weakness or strength in particular subjects; she might want more time for maths and less for English. It could be just the reverse for another child who is strong in mathematics. Once the number of days for each subject has been decided upon, note them down on the timetable.

Now, using the 'reverse approach', ask the child to first prepare for the subject whose exam is the last on the timetable. Gradually, the child should work her way up till she approaches the first subject for examination. The advantage of this method is obvious—closest to the examinations, the child will be preparing for the subject that is the first on the schedule. Its study will be fresh in her memory, with no extra time needed for its revision. The second paper, too, will be easier on the child as she had studied it just before this one, and so on.

5. Logistical help. Parents of young children are quite attuned to regularly carrying out little chores for them so it should not be very different or difficult for them to continue doing so now, during their exams. It is with older children, who generally operate independently, that parents need to make an extra effort to look after their requirements at this time.

Some children prefer studying late, while others prefer the early hours. Whatever it be, you must be willing to look after their needs. If the child is studying late, you can make a hot beverage for her, or give her a glass of juice with extra glucose in it. The brain is the most prolific consumer of glucose and needs a lot of energy to function optimally. So keep this fact in mind and fix small but calorie-rich mini meals for your child while she concentrates on her studies.

Waking up early to study requires strong willpower. Sometimes the child will feel tired and lethargic and will snooze through the alarm, or even worse, switch it off.

When she finally gets up an hour or two later, she will feel anxious or depressed at having lost precious study-time. This will adversely affect her entire day's schedule. To prevent this state of affairs, ask her what time she plans to get up in the morning. Let her set the desired alarm, but you set another one for yourself too. In the morning when your alarm goes off, go and check whether the child is awake; in case not, gently wake her up. You can give her some ten to fifteen minutes extra time to sleep, and then again request her to wake up.

For working parents who are perpetually deprived of sleep, this is a tough ask, but you should not hesitate to make this sacrifice during your child's exams. The joy of her success will make you forget all the hardships. The parent who is the early riser should take the responsibility of waking up the child with biscuits, toast, milk, tea, or whatever she prefers.

6. Moral support. The inherent stress associated with exams can upset even the most level-headed and brightest of students. There will be phases when they will feel vulnerable and depressed. During these periods of self-doubt, parents must provide them with moral support and help to boost their confidence. Lack of parental involvement can lead to the child developing feelings of inadequacy.

If the child is feeling uncertain, take out the mark sheets of previous exams in which she has done well and stick them on the wall near her study table. Seeing them will reassure her and fill her with the hope that she can repeat her successes again. Notions of success and failure, both, are manifestations of the games that our minds play on us, after all.

Finally, in our highly competitive society, where we compete for almost everything and practically anything, achievement of good academic grades by the child tops the priority list of every parent. Outstanding students get into good institutions and better jobs—this is the dream and motive of all parents. However, this desire can also lead to anxiety and failure if wrong approaches and techniques are adopted at the very beginning of a child's academic career. Parents must try to imbue regular and independent study habits in their wards. At the same time, they should avoid being overzealous, or the child may develop a pathological revulsion towards studies.

14

Smart Parenting

Parenting is an art that relies heavily on the use of common sense. How your children grow up will depend not just on how much care you give them, or the amount of money you spend on them, but on your smartness quotient as a parent. Your efficiency in tackling everyday matters is the key determinant to your child's success.

All parents want their children to succeed in life. For this, they must act with responsibility, restraint, equanimity, and patience. They must be clear and firm while dealing with their children, but not at the cost of a warm, loving, and mutually gratifying relationship.

1. Begin early

There is not much difference between raising a child, and building a skyscraper. If the first few storeys are out of alignment no one will notice; but when the structure is twenty to thirty storeys high, everyone will see that it tilts. So if you didn't do your job as a parent properly in the early formative years, the chances are you will end up with a leaning tower of Pisa, which you will need to support for the rest of your life.

From the very beginning you must try to instil good habits and values in your child. This is easier said than done! One of the most significant ways children learn correct and incorrect behaviour is by watching their parents. So be careful—you are their first and foremost role models and sooner or later they will imitate your actions and behaviour. As a first step, you will have to practise what you preach.

You can't sleep late and expect your child to wake up early, or go to bed without brushing your teeth and hope that she will brush hers before sleeping. You can't expect your child to speak the truth while you often lie unabashedly on your phone. If you shout to get your way, expect your children to do the same, or if you remain sprawled on a sofa watching television instead of finishing urgent household chores, they will also learn to defer doing their homework.

If you want to inculcate a reading habit in your child, start reading yourself, and if you want her to say 'sorry' and 'thank you', better start using these words yourself. When your child sees you apologising for a mistake, she will quickly learn to do the same.

2. Keep yourself well informed

It is most helpful for parents to keep themselves abreast of the latest trends, gadgets, and gizmos, especially in the children's areas of interest. Lagging behind in this cyber age, where all knowledge is available on the World Wide Web, will not go down well with them.

You may not like the noise created by rock bands, but you can try to remember the names of a prominent few; if you don't know the names of all the movie stars, you can certainly discuss and praise the good Hollywood films. There is no need to master all the functions on the Apple iPhone 5S, but there is no harm in being familiar with popular apps like Whatsapp. It's a good means of remaining in touch, and sharing happy photos and jokes with your children.

3. Conserve your energy

All of us have a certain reserve of physical and mental energy for dealing with the everyday activities and stresses of life. Unnecessary conflicts tend to drain this resource, and reduce the buffer to help us cope.

This means that one has to choose one's battlegrounds wisely. Sit down with your child and share your key issues with her; then, frame a set of guidelines for her and channellise your energy into seeing that they are followed. If you keep reacting to trivial issues, you will have little energy left to deal with the more important problems.

We will try to explain this by equating energy to money. Decide whether an issue is worth ₹10, ₹100, or ₹1,000, then spend your energy in accordance with that notional value of the issue. Overspending can only lead to an early burn-out.

If your child spills a glass of milk, think of the following possibilities before you start hollering:

1. Was it a mistake? If yes—you don't have any right to shout; even you can make a mistake.
2. Was it deliberate? If yes, think about the cost—if ₹10, it is negligible. The only issue worth dealing with is the indiscipline of the child. Talk to her and explain the inappropriate behaviour, also warn her of unpleasant consequences in future.

4. Saying no is important

I had gone out for dinner with a family I know very well. As we came out of the restaurant, their five-year-old son Aryan saw a hawker selling toy cars. He demanded a particular car, and when refused, started whining, then wailing, and finally shrieking with rage. In order to stop him, his parents were tempted to buy him the car, but their momentary hesitation gave me the opening I was looking for. I told them to deal with the situation firmly and not to succumb to the child's irrational demand.

On the way back, Aryan's cries continued, drowning the car stereo by many a decibel, but by the time I dropped them off at their gate, his cries had changed to a whimper. Later, I was informed that Aryan was off to sleep the moment he was put to bed, and when he got up in the morning had forgotten all about the car.

Children are the worst victims of the advertising blitzkrieg on television; new toys, dolls, chocolates, electronic games, and bicycles fire their imaginations and increase their cravings. They are easily sold to new ideas and products and, when unable to acquire them, become frustrated.

The primary reason for parents giving in to their children's unreasonable demands is to avoid a 'scene'; it's the easiest way out. If your child manages to have her own way every time, by crying, pleading, or pestering, she will quickly master the technique and make your life a misery. Not only will the demands increase as she gets spoilt; they will become more and more irrational.

When your child is creating a scene in a shop, it is better to ignore it. Once you say 'no', it should remain a firm NO! Stand by your decision, even if her tantrum makes you look heartless. She must learn that crying and cajoling, throwing herself on the floor and yelping, will not achieve anything. If necessary catch hold of her and leave the shop—sometimes you have to be rigid to prove a point.

Don't buy expensive gifts in a casual manner. From the very beginning make it clear to your children that whatever you buy for them, or for yourself, involves serious decision-making. If your child wants a new bicycle and you feel it is justified, you should say: 'Although you do need a new bicycle, we will still have to discuss what kind of bicycle to buy. You can't go to the market and pick one up just like that.'

If your daughter demands a new pair of party shoes, and you know she doesn't need them, don't beat about the bush by saying that they appear flimsy, or are not worth the price, or that having so many shoes is unjustified. Such reasoning may sound okay to an adult, but it is beyond the comprehension of a child. You should try to offer the simplest explanation for your refusal; simply tell her: 'You don't need any shoes.'

Parents must guide their children to strike a balance between unreasonable demands and reasonable fancies, and about better ways of raising their demands and having them fulfilled. Your job is to help your children understand what's worth getting and what isn't, and that many things are useless and not worth buying. They must get the message that money is not an unlimited commodity, and that it must be spent wisely. If you use prudence—even in indulgence—it will not harm your child.

5. Don't over-instruct the child

Whether at home or away, some parents are in the habit of handing out continuous and unnecessary instructions to their child. An occasional emphasis on basic norms of behaviour and etiquette is okay, but constant nagging over standing straight, sitting properly, saying bye-bye, sorry, and thank you, can prove counterproductive.

More often than not, parents bringing their kids to my clinic seem to mistrust their ability to follow my simple instructions while examining them. They repeat everything I say: 'stand on the weighing scale, sit on the revolving stool, open your mouth wide, put out your tongue, breathe deeply...' When I ask children to take deep breaths some parents even go to the length of asking them to pump their chests like Baba Ramdev does while doing yoga!

This way, the parents only add to the confusion and make the already apprehensive child panicky. Their lack of confidence in her can also lead to the development of feelings of insufficiency; the child will start depending on the parents to take all her decisions for her, and in the long run might develop an inferiority complex.

So don't fall into the trap of being an over-smart, overbearing parent. Let your child fumble and falter and do things her way, without your interference. She is bound to learn sooner than later, and once she learns through her own efforts, she is not going to forget the lessons ever.

6. Let children take charge

You can't teach 'responsibility' but you can make a child 'responsible'. Eleven-year-old Ayushman was an incorrigible little brat—lazy, irritable, and generally disinterested in the world around him. He loved to watch 'any-damn-thing' on television, and his only contribution in the home was to keep it in a state of a perpetual mess.

Ultimately, his parents decided to involve him in running the home. He was made responsible, under their guidance, for purchasing the monthly groceries. At the beginning of each month, he was given the sum of money required to cover the monthly expenditure on groceries. He was also provided with a diary to maintain the record of purchases. Any unspent amount, at the end of the month, went into his kitty. This exercise helped his arithmetic grades and bank balance, both, to improve substantially.

Today Ayushman has no time for television—he is an avid young businessman instead, one who has learnt to save and to spend wisely.

7. Exude positivity and optimism

Parents must look at the brighter side of the child, and highlight her competencies and accomplishments. Focusing on the weaknesses and blaming her for minor lapses can boomerang. When they use praise and rewards, instead of criticism and punishment, parents generally obtain positive results, are able to eliminate undesirable behaviour, and reinforce good habits in their children.

Yamini, aged fourteen, was brought to my clinic with

complaints of general weakness and poor memory. She was unable to remember anything and was performing poorly in her studies. Her parents had already administered her with a variety of the so-called 'memory enhancing tonics', but to no effect.

While talking to her, I was pleasantly surprised by her clear and precise diction. Her parents said that she had always spoken like this, even as a little girl.

I enquired if she had ever participated in a speech competition or debate and the answer was in the negative. I suggested that she should enter her name for such an opportunity whenever it came her way.

At the end of the consultation I wrote out two prescriptions. Yamini's prescription contained an iron tonic, as she was mildly anaemic. Her parents' prescription was:

1. Motivate Yamini to participate in a speech competition or debate.
2. Give her 100 per cent support—emotional as well as material—when she decides to participate.

Two months later, a beaming Yamini entered my clinic with her parents. She was holding an impressive-looking trophy in her hands, having won it in an inter-school speech competition on the topic 'Eliminate Child Labour'. She had stood first among fifty-odd children from eighteen leading schools of the city. No doubt, her parents had helped her in writing the speech, but it was Yamini who delivered it—and with aplomb.

The victory gave a tremendous boost to Yamini's confidence and she started developing faith in her abilities. This began to reflect in her improved academic performance, and her 'memory problem' became a thing of the past.

8. Heads I win—tails you lose

Choose two options that are both acceptable to you, and ask the child to pick the one she prefers. Whatever the child's decision, it leaves you happy and smiling. For example, ask the child whether she would like to study at night for the exam or get up early in the morning. Either way you ensure that your child prepares for the exam. If instead of 'either' the child replies 'neither', remind her that 'neither' is not an option and she has to choose from the two offered options. Just hold on to your nerves and your child will make a choice within a few minutes.

If you adopt an open-ended approach and ask the child: 'When would you like to study for your exam?' you may either get no response or one that is not acceptable to you. Smart parents make it appear that it is the child who is making the choice.

9. Don't act like a detective

You return home from work and switch on the TV for the latest news, but the screen of your latest acquisition—a

42-inch LED set—remains dark. You had left it in perfect working condition in the morning. You call your children, and pointing to the TV, thunder, 'Who did it?' Your children vehemently deny having come anywhere near it, making it almost impossible to find out 'who did it', as they keep blaming each other.

Children are driven by curiosity, and by a spirit of adventure. If, and when, this turns into a 'misadventure' is a matter of your luck. The question: 'who did it', creates a situation where the child feels cornered, and the fear of punishment makes her point an accusing finger at a sibling or a servant. By asking 'who', you convey your intention to discover and punish the guilty party. So whether the child has done it or not she will usually answer 'not me', and try to shift the blame onto others.

If, instead, you ask, 'How did it happen', you will have a better chance of getting the response you need. Call your children and point out the problem. If they accuse each other, tell them you are not interested in knowing who did it, but in knowing why the television is not working. Your children are sure to feel bad about damaging it, and are likely to be more responsible in future.

Finally, it may even turn out that your TV simply blew a fuse, and there was absolutely no need for you to have blown yours as well.

10. Avoid being a 'super parent'

Apoorv was launched on the path of success from the moment his umbilical cord was cut. When he was a little baby, his father fortified him with a multitude of multivitamin syrups, while his mother tried to strengthen his body by massaging him with extra virgin olive oil.

Now, his parents strive hard to ensure that he always stands first, whether it is in academics, sports, dancing, painting, singing, or debating. While talking to Apoorv, their favourite words are: 'vital, urgent, significant, important, at the end of the day'. They ferry him to endless tuitions and coaching sessions throughout the day. The evenings are again devoted to achieving academic excellence.

Yes! Apoorv's parents are 'Super Parents' and they want him to be a 'Super Kid'. They have unlimited energy and are so highly charged that they just can't relax. Their devotion to the success of their child can render an inferiority complex to us 'ordinary', 'normal' parents. By watching the way they operate—always at full throttle—we may sometimes feel forced to verify our own antecedents and credentials as 'good' parents.

'Super Parents' are so busy running around 'doing things for' their children that they miss out on 'being *with*' their children. They get trapped in their own frantic drive to succeed, and fail to forge an emotional and mental bond with them. Their exacting standards and demands for perfection put extreme pressure on their children, who start feeling guilty and unworthy if they fail to live up to the super expectations of their super parents. Thus, unknowingly, parents make their children anxious and unhappy.

Some people may argue in favour of 'Super Parents', but they should sit back and think awhile! Who is benefiting from these efforts? Is your own need for glory reaping misery on your child? Is she being sacrificed at the altar of your ego? If yes, then perhaps it's time for you to drop the facade of being a 'Super Parent' and begin sincere efforts at becoming a 'Normal Parent'.

11. Learn to stay calm

One of the very best ways to become a better parent is to batter your anger and not your child. It's hard to think clearly when you're angry, and you might forget every sensible thing you know about good parenting. Try to remember your own childhood—its trials and its joys—to avoid situations getting complicated. Children will make mistakes; they will do silly, mischievous, or thoughtless things. At such times, take a few deep breaths and try to calm down. As parents you must maintain your cool and exemplify adult dignity.

15
CAN—Child Abuse and Neglect

A closely-guarded secret, child abuse has been present in all societies for centuries, but its impact in the present-day context, with both parents working, has increased manifold. In recent years, it has been the subject of extensive studies by social scientists, psychologists, and paediatricians. We will look at some important aspects of child abuse, and how it undermines a child's true potential.

It is a misconception that child abuse is restricted to the lower socio-economic strata of society. Children from seemingly 'perfect' middle and upper class homes are by no means exempt from this malady; they too, face physical violence, emotional trauma, and sexual exploitation. Even the 'prestigious' schools of the affluent are a breeding ground for such abuse of children. The difference is more of degree and frequency than an absolute one.

The perpetrators of violence or sexual abuse are often

'trusted' individuals, usually male family members in a position of authority. The children, who are victims, can themselves become abusers in later life. They may be physically violent to children in their care or to their own children.

CAUSES OF ABUSE

1. Lack of parenting skills, particularly the ability to respond to a young child's developmental needs, combined with unrealistic expectations for the stage of the child's development often results in physical violence.
2. Cultural acceptance of corporal punishment and inherent violence within the society greatly affects the incidence of child abuse.
3. An unwanted child, especially in the background of financial pressures and unemployment, is at high risk for abuse.
4. Unsupported and socially isolated, single-parent homes can become haunted with the cries of abused children.
5. Child abuse is a natural corollary of 'substance abuse' on the part of parents. There is a strong association between an alcoholic father and domestic violence/sexual abuse.
6. Child abuse is almost a certainty when parents themselves have been abused and neglected as children.

EFFECTS

1. The susceptibility of a child to abuse, and its health consequences, are dependent upon the child's age and stage of development—the younger the child, the more devastating the impact.
2. Abusive experiences, especially when multiple and prolonged, generally have a deleterious effect on the physical and mental well-being of the child.
3. Abused children exhibit anxiety and avoidance behaviour. They may become detached from their surroundings, withdrawing into a shell, or manifest highly aggressive behaviour.
4. One of the common legacies of child abuse in any of its forms is low self-esteem. Such children fail to achieve their potential in almost any field of life.

PHYSICAL ABUSE

About 5 to 10 per cent of children experience physical violence. Every year several children are brought to government hospitals or private health-care facilities as a consequence of abuse.

Few, if any, parents ever admit to physically abusing their children. Many a time they come up with the most improbable stories regarding their children's injuries. Whatever the precipitating cause, it is the basic lack of parenting skills that leads to physical violence. Such parents are busy with their own lives, and instead of getting involved with their children, neglect them. When the child seeks their attention, they get irritated and resort to verbal and physical abuse. Some callous parents use children as 'punching bags' and let loose fierce punches at the slightest provocation.

The spectrum of injuries as a result of physical abuse is very wide. Starting from simple bruises and minor cuts it may extend to neurological damage and physical disability. Children who are brain-damaged, mentally retarded, blind (retinal detachment), or deaf (damage to the eardrum) as a result of physical violence, are obviously at a disadvantage. Coupled with low self-esteem, these injuries can prevent them from any worthwhile achievement.

EMOTIONAL ABUSE

As compared to physical and sexual abuse, emotional abuse is harder to define and almost impossible to prove. What may be termed as abuse in one culture could well be an acceptable child-rearing practice in another. Emotionally abused children have significant impairment of mental and emotional functioning. They may suffer from anxiety, depression, withdrawal, or aggression. Compromised mental growth can lead to delayed development.

If children are repeatedly told that they are 'dumb', 'stupid', 'good for nothing', or 'retarded', they are likely to come to believe what they are told, especially when it is the parents who utter these words. Once children develop a feeling of worthlessness, it becomes part of their self-image. It is no exaggeration to say that these children will end up as failures since, from the very beginning, they have been made to feel so.

Parents cause emotional injury by:

1. *Rejection.* Parents refuse to look after the needs of their child and do not acknowledge her worth. This is an active form of neglect.

2. *Ignoring.* Here, the parents fail to involve themselves in the child's activities, depriving her of essential stimulation, thus, subverting her emotional growth and intellectual development. This is a passive form of neglect.

3. *Taunting.* Inappropriate criticism, humiliation, ridicule, or accusations undermine a child's self-esteem and cause grievous damage to her personality.

4. *Terrorising.* Parents create an atmosphere of fear through their malignant shouting and cursing. Constant threats and verbally abusive assaults make the child tense and insecure and erode her self-image.

5. *Mal-socialising.* Some parents hinder the normal socialisation process of the child by preventing her from making friends. Others may go to the extent of inducing the child to engage in destructive antisocial activities.

6. *Failing as role models.* Parents who are chronic alcohol or drug abusers, or prone to domestic violence, generally end up as social outcasts. Perpetually in a financial mess, they may suffer from stress and various other psychological disorders. The prevailing tension in such homes stifles the child's personality.

SEXUAL ABUSE

Sexual abuse of children, and its impact on their psychosocial and intellectual growth, has been the subject of increasing attention during the last two decades. Estimates of its prevalence may not be very accurate because the associated social and legal implications lead to gross under-reporting.

Sexual intercourse with a child by an older person is the most extreme form of abuse, but 'inappropriate fondling' or 'dirty talk' also constitutes sexual abuse. Girls are the common victims, and the perpetrators generally family members, or people well known to the family. The abuse may start when the child is quite young, even in the preschool stage, and could continue for years. As the child grows and starts understanding relationships in their proper perspective, the enormity of her aberrant circumstances dawns on her. She is faced with several distressing questions:

- Who should she tell?
- Will anyone believe her?

- Was it her fault?
- Will her family break up if she tells?
- Will the abuser be punished or jailed?

The perpetrator may threaten the child with dire consequences if she were ever to spill the beans to anyone. Alternatively, the abuser may try to please her with gifts. He may tell her that they have a special relationship; that it is to be their own secret to be shared with no one else. Some common lines used by sexual abusers are, 'You are my little princess. You are the nicest little girl.' In her agony and confusion, the child hesitates to disclose the abuse, and may never tell anyone about it.

Although there are several physical effects of sexual abuse, like rupture of the hymen, tears and lacerations in the vaginal and anal areas, sexually transmitted diseases, and pregnancy, it is the psychological and emotional repercussions that are the most difficult to overcome . If it is a brief episode the child may prevail over the trauma, but if it continues through much of her childhood, the damage to her psyche is more permanent.

The conflict faced by sexually abused children is complex and agonising. Their self-esteem suffers serious damage, which leads to failures in many areas of life. The emotional consequences of abuse adversely affect their academic performance, and their ability to form and maintain healthy relationships, especially with the opposite sex.

Sexually abused children suffer from feelings of guilt because they believe that it was, at least in part, their fault that the abuse occurred. They may develop anger and hatred, directed primarily towards the abusing adult, or towards the parent who failed to protect them or refused to believe them when told about the abuse. When these children try to suppress their anger they become frustrated and depressed, and may develop suicidal tendencies. Sexually abused children may themselves become abusers of other children in later life.

Effect of sexual abuse

1. Low self-esteem
2. Depression
3. Suicidal tendencies
4. Running away from home
5. Absenteeism from school
6. Alcohol or drug abuse
7. Promiscuity, compulsive masturbation
8. Physical violence
9. Delinquent and criminal behaviour
10. Becoming child abusers themselves

WHAT CAN BE DONE

- Teasing out the effects of specific abusive experiences is often difficult or impossible. The best option is to plan interventions that can prevent abuse from taking place.

- Understanding the developmental needs of children and adolescents, and recognising their vulnerability to abuse, is a step in the right direction.
- Promotion and support of the healthy development of children and adolescents is a prerequisite.
- Strengthening the capacity and resilience of the families is a necessity.

Pick your nanny carefully. This is one measure that working parents must take. A family came to me with the complaint that their child had become abnormally dull. 'He keeps sleeping when I come home from office, and he hardly eats anything,' the mother told me in a distraught tone. After carefully examining the child I asked, 'Since when have you noticed these changes?' 'After I employed a young woman to look after him in my absence,' replied the mother. I examined the child carefully and found that he appeared to have been drugged. I told the parents to get a CCTV installed in the child's room.

My suspicion proved correct.

Soon after the parents had left for work, leaving the child in the care of the young woman, a man arrived and added something to the child's milk. Then leaving him there, sleeping, they went to another room. The parents confronted the woman with the CCTV footage and threatened to hand her over to the police. The woman started to cry and told them that it was her lover who was giving 'afeem' (opium) to the child.

Plenty of off-the-shelf sedatives are available, and an unscrupulous babysitter can use any of them. Sexual abuse of a girl child can also take place in the absence of working parents. One universal precaution that all working parents should take is to never employ a male servant to take care of their female child. Several instances of old and trustworthy male servants abusing girl children have been reported. Not only this, but both male and female same-sex abuse is also prevalent in these circumstances.

Child abuse is a social problem and each sector of society has an important role to play in its prevention. There is a need for national programmes for the prevention of child abuse, as well as for interventions that can help both—the victims and their families. Police, judicial authorities, and other agencies involved in investigating child abuse—particularly sexual abuse—need to be sensitive. They should be trained in procedures for information collection that preserve the dignity of the child, and do not cause more trauma.

For optimal growth and realisation of their full potential, children need the warm, nurturing, and affirming atmosphere of a stable, united family. They require love, care, and praise from their parents. They must be told that they are worthwhile individuals, with merits and virtues to become successful in life. Children need to feel safe, secure, and at peace with their world. They should get opportunities to interact, and develop satisfying relationships, with not only their parents and family members, but also with their teachers and other significant persons in their lives. A caring and supportive family environment can counter the potentially adverse effects of traumatic and stressful experiences.

16
Single Parenting

Worldwide, there has been a general increase in children living in single-parent homes. No contemporary book on parenting can do without a discussion on this scenario. Although most of the guidance and tips provided in this book also hold good for single parents, there are some issues which merit special mention.

Being a single parent, bearing most of the day-to-day responsibilities of raising the child, can be difficult, but not unrewarding. Single parents, and their children, face certain challenges, but there are also positive aspects.

REASONS BEHIND SINGLE PARENTING

Parents may be single by choice or by circumstance. Previously, the death of the spouse was the major cause for single parents; now divorce seems to have overtaken it. Other reasons include choosing this lifestyle, or having been in a relationship when the child was born, or being abandoned by their partner. In the US, a substantial number of cases are from out-of-wedlock pregnancies. Child Abuse & Neglect (CAN) can also be a reason for the child living with the separated non-abusive parent. Additionally, adoption is sometimes an option for single adults who want children.

In cases of divorce, children live with their 'custodial parent' or 'primary caregiver', usually the mother, and have visitation rights or a secondary residence with their 'non-custodial parent' or 'secondary caregiver', usually the father. Court cases for the custody of children can turn ugly, affecting them in many ways, and counselling is recommended for them.

MOTHER VS FATHER AS A SINGLE PARENT

'I am a single mother, and have been for about five years now. I have two boys who are full of energy. When I am tired and weak, I feel like a bad mother. I wonder what it is like to have no kids. My boys are good most of the time even in this situation, but they fight a lot among themselves. I am trying hard to provide for them, but their wants are never ending. When they act up, they make me really angry and sad. Yes, my life is hectic almost every day. I often wonder how I have been doing this all alone. There were many nights that I put myself to sleep crying. I am scared and lonely, but I also know I have to keep going for myself and my boys.'

This is the story of a single-parent (mother) family. Mothers as single parents are more common than single fathers. More than half the households in the US are now headed by single mothers, roughly 40 per cent by couples and the remaining by single fathers. Our own metro cities are also increasingly witnessing this phenomenon. Probably Bollywood has a role to play, both on and off screen.

Single mothers are better able to manage their jobs, households, and children, all, quite efficiently and successfully, because they have been conditioned into doing so, even while living with their spouse. Their closer bonding and natural nurturing instincts makes them the first choice for childcare, especially true if the child still needs nursing. In spite of all this, our society looks down on them, and, quite often they also face mental torture and sexual exploitation at work.

Single fathers, on the other hand, are considered martyrs. Traditionally, they were not the primary caregivers, they were the providers. This position has changed in recent years, with many fathers now playing an active parental role. It is not uncommon to find a stay-at-home dad, as the mother becomes the sole provider to the family. In such a set-up the father bonds and connects with the child more than the mother does.

DIFFERENCES BETWEEN SINGLE AND DUAL PARENTING

Single parenting differs from dual parenting in many ways, but the most common difference is the way in which the parent interacts with the child. In dual-parenting families, the mother and father usually decide together how to run the household. In a single-parent family, children are likely to be included in the discussion regarding major purchases or vacations.

Children of single parents may have more duties and responsibilities around the home from an earlier age, simply because there is no other adult present to bear them. Single parents feel stressed because they are doing the job of two people and after all, there are only twenty-four hours in a day. To top it all, they are expected to be the perfect parent, so good that the child doesn't feel the absence of the other missing parent.

PROBLEMS FACED BY SINGLE PARENTS

- The excessive workload a single parent faces can be truly taxing. Managing a child and a job is a daunting task because both are full-time occupations. Waking up the child in the morning, getting her ready for school, preparing her breakfast, dropping her to school or to the bus stop, going to work, bringing the child back in the evening, supervising her homework, arranging dinner, finishing a thousand odd jobs around the house, paying of bills—the list is endless. It requires

a superhuman effort to keep going, day in and day out, without a breakdown.
- The constant stress of being the ideal parent can take its toll, leading to irritability and maybe even depression.
- Single parents may suffer from a feeling of guilt over having failed to provide a complete family for their children, compromising their present, and maybe their future as well. The single parent can feel aggrieved if the child envies friends with both parents.
- It has been observed that the child is more likely to misbehave with the parent who she lives with, rather than the one who lives away. This is so because the resident parent is the day-to-day disciplinarian. Disciplining is no popularity pageant and differences and dissensions are bound to arise. Being awarded the 'bad person' tag by your child is a distinct possibility.
- Nurturing new relationships may be difficult for the single parent if the child is suspicious or jealous of the new person.
- A lonely single parent may cling to the child for support and company, making it difficult for the child to eventually leave home.

PROBLEMS FACED BY CHILDREN OF SINGLE PARENTS

- The need for 'extra hands' around the house can deprive the child from playing or simply hanging out

with friends. Participating in peer groups and developing interpersonal relationships is of extreme importance for the future development of the child.
- In cases of divorce, problems start for the child at the point of separation, when he has to live with a single parent. Being used to the presence of both—the mother and the father—the child finds it difficult to adjust to the constant absence of one parent. It is indeed a traumatic situation, and can lead to depression in the child.
- The child may feel torn between the two parents and obliged to take sides. This is especially the case if the parents are hostile towards each other.
- By and large, children in single-parent families, especially when living with the mother, have a near-equal say in the household. Because they have come to expect an equal status with an adult, they may clash with teachers and other authorities who demand unquestioning obedience. This can adversely affect their academic grades in school.
- These children are more likely to develop an inferiority complex when they compare themselves with children from homes with both parents and dual incomes.
- In homes where the father is the missing parent, children show a greater incidence of delinquency, addictions, and criminal behaviour.

POSITIVES FOR SINGLE-PARENT FAMILIES

Although single-parent homes have some handicaps, there are also some positives:

- The relationship between the parent and child is a close one.
- The child is typically mature and responsible.
- The parent is typically self-reliant and confident.
- Single parents tend to rely on positive problem-solving strategies rather than punishment, when faced with difficult child behaviour.
- Gender-specific roles (girls are supposed to do certain things and boys others) are less likely to be followed in single-parent families.
- Single fathers are more inclined to use non-punitive measures to deal with childhood misdemeanours, while those living with their spouse tend to punish the child more often.
- A child from a single-parent home who is loved and cared for, develops at par with a child from a dual-parent home.
- Constructive use of time, for example, reading, playing sports and so on, is not an issue as this depends on discipline and family routine, rather than on the presence of one or both parents.

Here are some stray but revealing thoughts shared by a girl raised by a single father:

Single Parenting

'Life with a single father wasn't anything different, or special, or traumatising—though I could see the concern in people's faces when I said that my sister and I grew up with a single father. With a combination of sympathy and surprise they would ask in weird, hushed tones about my mother. I'd rattle off a response that I'd gotten used to saying for so long: "My parents are divorced," and then watch sympathy change to confused acceptance.

'We learnt independence earlier than most. My sister started doing her own laundry when she was nine years old. We stayed home alone by ourselves for long stretches of time while my father worked long hours at a string of jobs. When he worked the night shift, my sister and I handled ourselves, making sure the dog was fed, putting ourselves to bed at a decent hour, and getting prepped for school the next day.

'After I finished school I could not clear the competitive examinations for professional courses, and we had no money for the payment for seat or management quota admissions. I was a bitter, miserable troll, slumping around the house. I was deliberately, purposefully horrible, resentful of the fact that we somehow didn't have the money to send me to college, and full of a righteous anger at the fact that adequate provisions for my future were delayed.

'I think I only began to realise the fullness of the sacrifices our father made for us when, a few years later, my sister and I graduated with professional degrees. He announced that now, after raising us, he was getting remarried (to a woman that we did not think was good enough). I handled this news with a cool detachment, celebrating his happiness, but keeping my thoughts mostly in check. At the reception for his wedding, after a few glasses of wine, I saw how happy he was, and I realised that there will never be anyone good enough for the man who raised me.'

Now can you mark out any difference in the thoughts of this child vis-à-vis a child raised in a regular two-parent family?

DON'TS FOR A SINGLE-PARENT (DIVORCED) FAMILY

- Don't involve the child in marital disputes. All the discussions, discord, and arguments should take place in private.
- Don't make the child feel guilty for enjoying her time with the other parent.
- Don't fight during parental hand-overs of the child as it can put her under stress.
- Don't pester the child with questions about any special friend/partner present during her visit to the other parent.
- Don't admonish the child for taking a few hours/days to settle down again after visiting the other parent.

FINANCIAL PLANNING

Single parents need to be doubly careful with their finances—present and future. When you have only yourself to depend on, a solid financial plan could well be your best ally. In these times of price-rise, inflation, and job insecurity, it is difficult enough for a couple to manage the household expenses; for a single parent the task becomes doubly tough. Financial security can be achieved only if money is saved judiciously, and invested intelligently. Here are a few tips to attain this goal:

Life insurance. A wide variety of plans are available in the market. Choose the company and the plan that most suit your needs and resources. For life insurance, a term plan is preferred because it provides more cover at a lesser cost. It is advised that the sum assured should be ten times your annual income.

Medical insurance. Medical treatment is not cheap. While outpatient care is still manageable, admission in a hospital can prove expensive. A medical cover in the vicinity of five lakhs should take care of most emergencies. Treatment costs are going up constantly, and it would be prudent to include your child in the policy cover. Along with a medical insurance policy, a critical illness cover and an accidental disability rider should also be included.

Create a contingency fund. Emergencies crop up unannounced—you have an accident, someone in the family falls sick and needs your attention, or you lose your job. For such crises you should have an emergency fund in place, so that even if you are not earning, regular expenses are taken care of. The thumb rule is to keep aside at least three months' expenses in instruments with easy liquidity.

Provide for your child's education. Education, especially a professional course, is costly. Your plan to cover this will depend upon the child's aptitude and inclination. It is a good idea to invest in a long-term product when building a corpus fund for this requirement. It becomes even more compelling if the child intends to go abroad for higher education; you will have to factor in other costs such as lodging and boarding in addition.

Save for retirement. When you are in your thirties, retirement seems too far away, but actually this is the right time to start planning for that eventuality. You can invest in long-term instruments like regular income funds. A Provident Fund—the mandatory investment for working classes—and the PPF scheme are also good ways to build a post-retirement corpus, especially considering their tax benefits.

Make a will. What will happen to my child if I die? This question is never far from a single parent's mind. Writing a will is an important decision that should be taken early. You will need to have it registered, and to nominate someone as a guardian to execute the will if the child is a minor.

SOME HELPFUL SUGGESTIONS FOR SINGLE PARENTS

- Do not let your child develop an inferiority complex. Try your best to motivate her to develop normal relationships with peers. If the child is a boy, do not project him as the man of the house. A single mother should not repeatedly tell her son that he is 'Mummy's only support' and 'in future he is the one who will look after Mummy'. Even before blossoming, the little child's personality can get crushed under this heavy load of expectation.
- It is important that single fathers or mothers should not hold grudges against the opposite sex, nor should they provoke their children to do so. Holding a grudge will present a distorted picture of the world to the child, and he/she will develop a negative attitude towards relationships. Remember all humans are not alike.
- Single parents should not hesitate in taking help from their friends in times of need. Many of them have broken ties with their family because they have chosen their partner, or taken a divorce against their family's wishes. Even so, whenever the need arises, parents do come forward to help. When that happens, let them do it.
- It is the duty of the ex-husband to share the financial burden of running the household. In such matters the ex-wife should obtain legal advice. Certain government agencies can also help in resolving this issue.

- If you meet someone again, with whom you feel compatible, don't hesitate in giving yourself a second chance at a relationship. You never know—this may well be the happiness you have been searching for...

Acknowledgements

The inspiration to write this book came from Kapish Mehra, MD, Rupa Publications, who mooted the idea that new-age parents need a modern book on parenting. We put our thinking caps on and prepared the framework, and soon our efforts metamorphosed into this new-age parenting guide. Having previously written three successful books on this genre helped greatly in our endeavour.

No book can be written without utilising personal experiences and observations. The same stands true for us. For this we thank our parents—R.S. Kapur, Santosh Kapur, M.N. Tandon and Prabha Tandon, who helped us build a firm foundation of right values and meaningful education.

As we move ahead in life we meet people who amaze us with their soft, sweet core wrapped in a shell of level-headedness and clarity of vision. Mahesh Kumar Shah and Saroj Shah is one such couple who, we believe, most deserve to be put in the category of 'Smart Parents with Smarter Kids'.

It was great to have Ritu Vajpeyi-Mohan and Sneha Gusain of Rupa Publications in our team during the making of this book.

www.ingramcontent.com/pod-product-compliance
Lightning Source LLC
Chambersburg PA
CBHW070547170426
43201CB00012B/1749